In Search of Harmony

In Search of Harmony

A History of Bali Nyonga

Fondi Ndifontah Nyamndi

SPEARS ⑤ BOOKS
DENVER, COLORADO

Spears Books
An Imprint of Spears Media Press LLC
7830 W. Alameda Ave, Suite 103-247
Denver, CO 80226
United States of America

First Published in the United States of America in 2023 by Spears Books
www.spearsbooks.org
info@spearsmedia.com
Information on this title: www.spearsbooks.org/in-search-of-harmony

ISBN: 9781957296180 (Paperback)
ISBN: 9781957296197 (eBook)

Designed and typeset by Spears Media Press LLC
Cover designed by Doh Kambem
Cover Picture: The ritual Spears and Standards of Bali Nyonga (photo credit: author)

Distributed globally by African Books Collective (ABC)
www.africanbookscollective.com

Contents

ONE

Gawolbe and the Chamba Migrations   1

   Early Stages   7

   In Bamun Country   10

   In the Bamenda Grassfields   12

TWO

Break-Up of the Chamba Alliance   15

   Encounter with the Forest and the Swing Eastwards   15

   The Battle of Kolm and the Death of Gawolbe 16

   Separation   18

THREE

The Emergence of Bali Nyonga   23

   The Bali-BaTi Alliance   24

   The Bali-Bamun War, 1855   26

   Fonyonga's Reforms   27

   Bali Nyonga in the Bamenda Grassfields   31

   Final Settlement   32

FOUR

Consolidation of the Fondom   37

   Administration of the Realm   45

   Inter-Bali Rivalries   51

FIVE

The First Europeans 55

    Zintgraff in Bali 56

    Bali Nyonga in German Policy 63

    The Decline of Bali Influence 78

SIX

Later Europeans 87

    The First World War and the Coming of the British 88

    Bali Nyonga under British Rule 91

SEVEN

Assault on the Fondom 98

    The Coming of Galega II 98

    Background to the Unrest 101

    The Legal Impasse 104

    Attacks on the Realm 106

    Aftermath of the Crisis 107

EIGHT

Bali Nyonga Since Independence 112

    Bali Nyonga in Politics 112

    Resurgent Land Problems 114

APPENDICES

    Report of the Commission of Inquiry into the 1952 Riots 121

    Nigeria Order made under the Collective Punishment

    Ordinance N° 33 of 1952 (Cap. 34) 133

    The Manson Report 135

Selected Bibliography 155

Index 157

Illustrations

Figure 2.1 Gawolbe's Migrations   18

Figure 3.1 Fonyonga's Route   33

Figure 4.1 The Bali Nyonga Sphere in the 1870s and 1880s   41

Tables

Table 4.1 Bali Nyonga Tǎdmànjì in the Mid-19th Century   49

ONE

Gawolbe and the Chamba Migrations

The early 1800s witnessed intense activity in the lush plains of the Faro-Deo River system, in present-day north Cameroon, as successive groups elbowed one another in and out of the area.

First came the Chamba, a tall, negroid people with a distinctly imperious bearing, who occupied a series of villages in a place called Lamurde Jungum on the right flank of the river Faro. From there, they spread southwards into the Faro-Deo confluence and westwards across the Alantika mountains, an area that was later known as the Chamba homeland.

This homeland was occupied by two sets of Chamba peoples, differentiated linguistically and geographically. The Chamba spoke two main languages - Daka and Leko - which were close enough in vocabulary and grammar to form the same broad group, distinct from other neighbouring languages. These settlers were thus known either as Chamba Daka or as Chamba Leko, depending on which of the two languages they spoke.[1]

---

1   C.K. Meek has suggested that the terms Chamba Daka and Chamba Leko came about as a result of the fusion of three distinct peoples: the Chamba, the Daka and the Leko, with the Chamba serving as the common denominator in the fusion. C.K. Meek, *Tribal Studies in Northern Nigeria*, Vol. 1, (London: Kegan Paul, Trench and Trubner, 1931), p. 329 fn. Eldrigde Mohammadou claims that the Chamba Leko language was otherwise known as MUBAKO, the language spoken in many of the Chamba chiefdoms of the Bamenda grassfields. Eldridge Mohammadou, *Les Royaumes Foulbe du Plateau de l'Adamaoua XIX Siècle*, Institute for the Study of Languages and Cultures of Africa and Asia, Vol. IV, Tokyo, 1978, p. 34. But it is more probable that Mukabo was only a dialect of Chamba Leko.

Geographically, the Chamba homeland fell into two regions, east and west of the Alantika mountains. The Chamba Daka occupied the western part of the homeland, while the Chamba Leko occupied the eastern region between the Alantika mountains and the river Faro.

It appears that the early Chamba were animated by two contrasting migration tendencies: they were given to long, almost wandering migrations, yet they seemed to be a rather sedentary community, who did not exercise any of the activities normally associated with nomadic life.

The linguistic and geographical dichotomy of the early Chamba society has been the source of some controversy over the tribal nature and identity of the Chamba. It has been argued that they were not a tribe or kingdom as such but merely an agglomeration of villages with little in common. As it were, the Chamba did not have any overall authority or imperial centre which exercised control over the entire homeland. Chamba society consisted of small independent chiefdoms tenuously held together by the distinct "Chambaness" of each village. Among the Leko, these villages were governed by powerful chiefs called Gara or Ga, who were appointed from a clan known as Gatkuna. The royal matriclan, Gatkuna, from which Chamba Leko chiefdoms drew their leaders, thus constituted a sort of guarantor of tribal unity.

Otherwise, the Chamba were a well-organised community. They had many skills: they were adept blacksmiths, intrepid hunters, industrious farmers and careful breeders of small humpless cattle. By the standards of the neighbourhood, they led a life of great prosperity.

And they were capable warriors too: expert archers, also very skilled with the assegai, sword and buffalo skin shield called "pana." The art of warfare was part of their culture, carefully taught to children from the very early ages. A sheathed dagger concealed on an extra belt under their gowns was an integral part of the daily Chamba outfit, and they cunningly carried their spears as walking-sticks. Even in normal times, they were always well-armed.

Which was all very well because, in an age of the survival of the fittest, a people's fighting ability was perhaps its most valued skill. Prosperity often attracted career pillagers who roamed the land, looting their living from other people's efforts. It also attracted the envy of less fortunate neighbours, in regions where good land was scarce. The Chamba villages usually survived the fleeting attacks of looters, especially as these sought merely to reap what was ripe without disrupting the people's ability to produce more. They did not constitute regular armies. They were simple raiding bands, whose survival also depended on the prosperity of their victims. So their attacks, however frequent, were superficial and short-lived.

It was a different proposition when it came to opposition from neighbouring communities, who sought possession of the lands from which the Chamba derived their prosperity. In that case, the attacks were sustained, leading to the subjugation or migration of the vanquished people.

The Chamba were particularly vulnerable to this type of attack. The territorial organisation of the homeland, in which every village was independent, made it difficult for them to mobilise one large army to defend the homeland. In each emergency, Chamba disunity played into the hands of their enemies.

The first to expose the weaknesses of the Chamba were well-horsed Bata warriors from Demsa, who were attracted by the Chamba Leko settlements in the loft lower basins of the Faro. These were amongst the most coveted lands in the neighbourhood; they were also the easiest to attack and difficult to defend.

The shielded Bata horsemen mounted a series of assaults on the Chamba homeland, displacing its occupants in stages. They were forced up the valley of the Faro, fighting a fierce rear-guard resistance as they retreated. They finally found safety across the river where they founded a new settlement called Diddo, which the Fulani later renamed Chamba after them.[2]

But it was not long before the Bata arrived this new settlement. Nor could the Chamba resist them any better this time. Indeed, the second wave of Bata attacks appears to have been even more ferocious, forcing the Chamba southwards towards Koncha.

---

2   Eldridge Mohammadou, *Les Royaumes Foulbe du Plateau de l'Adamaoua au XIX Siècle*, Institute for the Study of Languages and Cultures of Africa and Asia, Vol. IV, Tokyo, 1978, p. 40.

Paradoxically, Bata conquest of the Chamba homeland left them in turn exposed to attack by the Fulani, who were soon to replace them as the predominant people in the neighbourhood.

The Fulani are best remembered in the Adamawa for what was later to be referred to as the Fombina or Adamawa jihad, the holy war by which the Fulani under their leader Modibo Adama, lieutenant of the Caliph of Sokoto, Uthuman dan Fodio, set out to conquer the area from Yola to Rey Bouba and convert it into a vast Moslem empire. The jihad began in earnest in 1809, when Modibo Adama returned from Sokoto with a flag of legitimacy from the Caliph.

Before the jihad, the Fulani of the lower Faro were simple herds-men who paid tribute to Bata chiefs for the use of their pastures. They detested the subjugation, and their chiefs met regularly to brainstorm. And once they were sure of their muscle, they decided that the Bata levies were so exorbitant as to amount to economic exploitation. They rose against their hosts and in a very short space of time completely nullified Bata influence in the region. They drove the Bata from Lamurde Jungum, and they drove them from Diddo, on which site they created the chiefdom of Chamba. Fulani state-formation in the Adamawa, later cemented during the jihad, had begun.

The Fulani uprising against the Bata did not spare the Chamba, even though relations between them had always been of a different nature. The Chamba and the Fulani were trading partners, exchang-ing their bows and arrows for bush guns from Maroua, Kishini and Garoua.

And they cooperated in other fields as well. The Fulani sought and obtained the services of leading Chamba arrowsmiths to teach them their trade. The Chamba were eager to collaborate with the Fulani, who had overrun the hated Bata.

But the Fulani had other ideas. Instead of returning their tutors at the agreed time, the Fulani kept them further and forced them to create a stockpile of bows and arrows with which they rose against the Chamba. It was an uneven war, in which the Fulani gained a starting advantage by divesting their opponents of the services of their best minds. The Chamba were further demoralised because they did not know what intelligence the Fulani had squeezed out of the captive arrowsmiths. They were sensible enough not to mount a suicidal resistance, preferring instead to retreat from the area. It was yet another episode in the saga of the Chamba Leko first finding and then losing their homeland. But this time, rather than hang about the outskirts of the lost territory as before, they migrated further afield in search of new peace, prosperity and glory. The Chamba dispersal, which the Bata had set afoot some twenty years before now received a decisive push.

That dispersal, which was to bring groups of Chamba into the middle Benue plains and the Bamenda grassfields, is one of the most significant phenomena in Chamba history. There has been a tendency, erroneous in our view, to regard it as a fall-out of the Fulani jihad. But the jihad proper did not reach the Faro-Deo with the establishment of the Lamidats of Koncha and Chamba until the 1830s, by which time the Chamba Leko had since left the region. In time and space, the dispersal could be regarded as the sum total of events that at first gradually displaced and then violently forced out the Chamba Leko from the Faro-Deo. The pre-jihadic conflict between the Fulani and the Chamba and the Bata-Chamba clashes before that were both major causes. The latter uprooted the Chamba Leko from their first home-land around Lamurde Jungum while the former displaced them from their subsequent home in and around Koncha. Both events turned the Chamba Leko into strangers and migrants.

But perhaps the most significant single cause of the dispersion was a natural disaster that overwhelmed the homeland prior to the Fulani uprising. For four harsh years, the homeland was struck by a scorching drought which precipitated a serious famine. This drought was probably the reason why the Chamba offered so little resistance to the Fulani, in contrast with the fierce opposition that they had given the Bata earlier on. They must have felt that a drought-stricken homeland was not worth much defending. And it has been suggested that the Chamba were thinking of moving on anyway. So rather than deplete their ranks in war with the Fulani, they chose to move out in a retreat which, once started, developed momentum of its own.

Even so, the dispersion was not an organised migration. There was no overall power structure to direct it. As the outcome of war and ecological disaster the dispersal was instead a panic reaction to changed circumstances, with every Chamba Leko group seeking its own safety and livelihood. Instead of moving out in a single throng, they constituted themselves into bands of mounted raiders, marauding southwards by different routes and extracting their subsistence from the peoples they came across.

Still, the Chamba Leko diaspora was a very elaborate movement indeed, involving several Chamba groups as well as their non-Chamba allies. They left the homeland in distress and in a haste, taking their children and womenfolk with them as a sign that they were not going to return. Nor did they have any precise destination in mind. They simply followed the wind, living from day to day, in search of what they hoped would be the promised land.

Among the first to leave the homeland were the Ndagambila [singular: Ndagha], otherwise known as Bà'nì, who departed from a series of villages on the right flank of the river Deo, upstream from the confluence with the Isselou,[3] under their leader Gawolbe. They raided southwards through Tibati, Banyo and Fumban, before settling in the Bamenda grassfields where they founded the chiefdoms of Bali Kumbat, Bali Nyonga, Bali Gangsin, Bali Gham and Bali Gasho. During this migration, they constantly increased and diversified their ranks by absorbing numbers of the Buti, Tikali, Ti, Kufad and a variety of smaller groups. They have come to be known collectively as Bali Chamba or Bali for short.

The Bali Chamba were probably the largest group of the migrating Chamba Leko. They were either the best warriors or the most warlike, because the entire migration was a chain of military campaigns, with one raid leading to the next. And even after they had settled in the Bamenda grassfields, the southermost area of Chamba occupation, it took them years to find peace, as much with their neighbours as among themselves.

Very little is known of Gawolbe's life prior to the Chamba Leko dispersion. Some Chamba oral traditions relate that his actual name

3   Ibid., p. 37.

was Wodbe and that he was the son of a Chamba Leko chief called Gangsin.

Indications are that Gawolbe had actually succeeded Gangsin before migrating from the Faro-Deo. His name itself gives a tangible clue to this supposition. "Gawolbe" in Chamba Leko means "chief from the water."[4] The name comes from Ga or Gara meaning chief, and Wula or Wolba or Wolbe meaning water. The water in question is thought to refer to the sacred lakes of Kolongti, in which Leko chiefs were cleansed at the time of their investiture.[5] Gawolbe was the sixth chief of the Ndagambila, after Gangsin, Ganyam, Gabanjang, Gatum-jang and the first Gawolbe.[6]

Gawolbe's band was essentially an army on the move. It was not a professional army as such since there were no career soldiers at the time. In fact, all able-bodied men were soldiers of some sort, and sometimes even the women were involved. Their operational strategy was simple: raiding columns dispersed from a central camp (some-times maintained for several months), after vanguards had spied and reported on suitable villages to be raided. The army's main concern was food and fodder, with the capture and exchange of enslaved people for needed goods as a secondary aim.[7] All this required both war and diplomacy, the execution of battle and the negotiation of peace. It also required careful organisation and maintenance of alliances, an art at which the Bali Chamba were later found to be quite adept.

Early Stages

Just as his point and time of departure from the Faro-Deo, Gawolbe's itinerary in the southward migration that followed is not entirely clear. It seems that his first port of call was Koncha, in the plain of Koutine, which he easily ransacked, incorporating into his army various little groups that Kaberry and Chilver have referred to

---

4   P.M. Kaberry, *Fieldnotes on Bali Nyonga*, 1960, Ms, p. 116.
5   Eldridge Mohammadou, op. cit., p. 39.
6   Isaac Fielding Pefok, "Nu ndzo fon Bani ka bini a," Oral Account of Bali History, given by Tita Nji II, 1934, p. 5.
7   E.M. Chilver, *The Bali Chamba of West Cameroon*, Report, 1964, p. 46.

as Buti-Koncha, Nabuli, Babele and Sugneba.[8]

Encouraged by his successes in Koncha, Gawolbe attacked the people of Nyam Nyam, driving them into the Galim mountains as he marched south-eastwards.[9] He swept through Tignere and reached the neighbourhood of Ngaoundere or Tibati. It is not exactly certain which, perhaps because the same Mbum people inhabited both villages. What is certain is that it was from among these Mbum that Gawolbe made his first major allies, a contingent later referred to as Kufad or Gbadineba.[10] These Kufad were one of the largest groups in Gawolbe's alliance. Their presence was further marked by Gawolbe's adoption of the "lama" or throwing knife, into the outfit and traditions of the Chamba, thereby initiating the cultural diversification of the alliance. It has been suggested that the name BALI, by which the Chamba chiefdoms of the Bamenda grassfields would later be known, evolved from the Kufad term Bare or Bari or Baari, their designation of Gawolbe's men and a probable corruption of Pere or Pyeri or Peli by which some of the invading Chamba called themselves.[11]

But the incorporation of the Kufad was not without a fight. The resistance of the Mbum was the first serious challenge to the migrating Chamba, enough to force Gawolbe to back off from the Mbum heartland and turn westwards towards Banyo instead.

There was to be neither peace nor tranquillity in Banyo. Hardly had they arrived than the Chamba were caught in the crossfire of a fratricidal conflict between the Buti chiefdoms of Mba and Mati, both branches of the Wute who were believed to have migrated from Bornu and founded the town of Banyo.[12] The support of the Chamba was enlisted by the Buti Mati to counterbalance the assistance that the Buti Mba were receiving from the Fulani. In the course of the fighting, a detachment of the Buti Mba, supported by Fulani cavalry sneaked through the mountain pass at Guenderou, and surprised the

8   Kaberry and Chilver, *Traditional Bamenda*, Buea, Government Printer, 1967, p. 16.
9   Eldridge Mohammadou, op. cit., p. 37.
10 Ibid.
11 Ibid. p. 103.
12 E.M. Chilver, op. cit., p. 20.

Mati and the Chamba from the rear,[13] forcing them out of Banyo and southwards through the kola trade route. In their common adversity, Gawolbe's band and the Buti of Mati became allies, the latter known for short as Buti.

Certain traditions do not entirely agree with this version of events, though. Some say that Gawolbe's alliance incorporated the Buti after conquering them in a ferocious battle around Mount Djoumbal in Banyo.[14] Others hold that the Buti themselves first incorporated the Kufad, and then voluntarily joined the Chamba together with them.[15] And still others suggest that, after a brief encounter at Koncha, presumably on the occasion when the Buti-Koncha were incorporated by Gawolbe, the Chamba and the Buti did not meet again until somewhere in the Bamileke grassfields where they joined forces willingly.[16]

But these traditions do not take account of the differences among the Buti and the conflict between them. They were not a homogeneous group against whom Gawolbe could have waged a single war or concluded a single peace. And the sheer size of the Buti contingent, and their quick rise to positions of prominence within the alliance and in later Bali chiefdoms, suggest that they could not have been captives of war. It is possible that Gawolbe might have fought an earlier war against the Buti of Mba, which explains why he so readily went into alliance with the Buti of Mati. Whatever the case, his departure from Banyo did not exactly have the trappings of a triumph.

Upon leaving Banyo, the Chamba alliance raided through Tikar territory, incorporating a group known as Tikali in circumstances not exactly remembered. They then overran the Kaka and went through Kovifem, the ancient capital of Nso,[17] before getting to the foot of the Bamun plateau where they coincidentally linked up with another group of migrating Chamba Leko, probably Gyando's, which had

13   Richard Fardon, *The Chamba: A Comparative History of Tribal Politics*, Unpublished Ph.D. Thesis, Vol. 2, London, 1980, p. 176.
14   Eldridge Mohammadou, op. cit., p. 103.
15   Richard Fardon, op. cit., p. 175.
16   E.M. Chilver, op. cit., p. 63.
17   J.P. Warnier, *Sociologie du Bamenda Précolonial*, Thèse de Doctorat, Université de Paris X, 1983, p. 299.

journeyed south through Gashaka and Mambila.[18] Together, presumably under Gawolbe's overall leadership, they mounted a bold attack on the Bamun.

In Bamun Country

Gawolbe's irruption unto the Bamun plateau took place in the early years of the nineteenth century, during the reign of the seventh Bamun chief, Ngu Moonzi. By then of course, the Bamun, though still a rather small chiefdom, were already well established on the plateau. This chiefdom, which the fiery chief Mbuombuo transformed by the mid-century into one of the most powerful in the entire grassfields, had been founded in the middle of the eighteenth century by an ambitious Tikar prince from Rifum called Nsa'ra.[19]

However, the founding of the Bamun chiefdom was followed by a long period of indolence, as one lethargic ruler after another mounted the throne. Their names are barely remembered in Bamun history.

It was in one of those undistinguished reigns that Gawolbe's mounted cavalry burst unto the Bamun plateau. Memories of that invasion have been handed down. The engagement was very brief: having been taken by surprise, the Bamun were thoroughly routed, and Ngu Moonzi escaped to Koundoum at the foot of the Nkogam mountains.[20]

What followed is not entirely clear. It is not known whether Gawolbe effectively occupied Fumban, and if so for how long. In fact, the duration of his stay in or around Fumban is a matter of some controversy. It has been suggested, quite mistakenly in our view, that the Chamba stayed in the Bamun neighbourhood until they were repelled by Mbuombuo in the mid-nineteenth century. But there were actually two Chamba visits to the vicinity of Fumban, the first by Gawolbe in the time of Ngu Moonzi, and the second by one of Gawolbe's successors, Fonyonga I, in the time of Mbuombuo, three Bamum reigns later. It has been possible to confuse both visits because

18   Eldridge Mohammadou, op. cit., p. 38.
19   Claude Tardits, *Le Royaume Bamoum*, (Paris: Armand Colin, 1980), pp. 97-99.
20   Ibid., p. 121.

the reigns of Bamun chiefs in those days were so short that in the roughly twenty years which separated Gawolbe's passage through Fumban from Fonyonga's return to the neighbourhood, as many as four rulers had come to the Bamun throne. Gawolbe was a contemporary to all four of them, and he and Fonyonga were coevals of Mbuombuo himself. No wonder, there has been the tendency to confuse the one Chamba ruler with the other, and Mbuombuo is sometimes thought to have raided Gawolbe, when in fact it was Fonyonga. Gawolbe and Mbuombuo actually never met, the former having died short of reaching Fumban on a second visit.

The circumstances of Gawolbe's departure from Fumban are also unclear. Bamun traditions recorded by Tardits mention a victory scored over the Chamba by one of Ngu Moonzi's princes, Nzi Mayup,[21] which precipitated their departure.

But Gawolbe did not leave alone. His short stay in the neighbourhood of Fumban had brought new hope to a number of groups who had suffered from Bamun conquest. Many followed him in small and large contingents.

The new Chamba allies from around Fumban included contingents from Sangaam, Sang, Ndiyang, Lap, Ngod Munyam, Kundem, Fuleng, Set and Dip.[22]

Gawolbe's departure from Fumban, situated around the early 1820s, took him first to Kuti, where the Ti gave him a very sympathetic reception. But he could not settle there without unseating his hosts, and Kuti was too close to Fumban for his own comfort. So Gawolbe moved on towards the Bamenda grassfields. According to Bali traditions collected by E.M. Chilver, the BaTi were so impressed by his fair-dealing leadership that many of them followed him. They were known, rather possessively, as Ti-Gawolbe, that is Gawolbe's BaTi.[23]

And not for the first time, Gawolbe left the scene of defeat much stronger than he had come. On leaving Fumban, his army was bigger and more diversified than it had been at any other time in the

---

21 Ibid.
22 E.M. Chilver, op. cit., p. 81
23 Ibid, pp. 70-71.

migration. In fact, the alliance had become so varied that internal distinctions began to appear. The most prominent of these divided the confederation into two broad groups — Bà'nì and Bǎnten or LoLo. The former was used to refer to the original Chamba confederates and their pre-Bamun adherents, while the latter served as a collective term for all those who joined the alliance after Fumban. In other words, the Bà'nì were composed of the Ndagambila and other Chamba elements, plus the Kufad, Buti and Tikali; the Bǎnten being the post-Fumban adherents of the Bà'nì.

The origins and purposes of the distinction are not known. Nor has it any clear-cut logic. The position of BaTi in the dichotomy seems both illogical and enigmatic. They are generally regarded as part of the Bà'nì group, even though they joined the alliance when Gawolbe was well clear of Fumban and although many groups incorporated immediately before or after them are wholly Bǎnten. The consideration of BaTi as Bà'nì rather than LoLo might have had to do with their origin from around Tibati, north-east of Fumban, which made them a distinctly "northern" people in relation to Fumban (like the other Bà'nì) and as opposed to the LoLo who came mainly from the vicinity of the Bamun capital or south of it.

With his army thus enlarged, Gawolbe left Kuti and crossed the river Noun into the Bamenda grassfields.

In the Bamenda Grassfields

Gawolbe burst into the Bamenda grassfields in the mid-1820s, with warlike intentions, marching and ravaging from place to place. His campaign was facilitated by the weakness of the opposition that he encountered: the chiefdoms of the Bamenda grassfields were generally small, many depleted by internal strife, and none capable of the muscle to withstand the Chamba. To many an indigene of those grassfields, the ruthless ferocity of the mounted Chamba warriors was simply too much. The "mbangtsu" or "red mouths" as they were called, in reference to their habit of chewing kola nuts, were a veritable terror in the grassfields. News of their presence spread like wildfire and many villages vacated their sites even before they arrived.

The military reputation of the Chamba had been earned by their expert cavalry, an elite corps of hardened fighters, which had gradually constituted itself into a more or less professional para-military force that conquered new lands and policed those lands while under Chamba occupation. Their defence role was far less prominent than their conquering mission. For, apart from the odd, often half-hearted counterattack, the Chamba did not have to worry about their own security, as very few groups were anxious to confront them. So, they just marched on. They seldom stayed in one place long enough to grow their own food, only long enough to consume what they found. And they were off again! As J.P. Warnier has observed, « *Les Tchamba n'etaient pas des marchands. C'etaient des pilleurs, des ravageurs de provinces. Ils repugnaient d'acheter ce qu'ils pouvaient prendre.* »[24]

It was not long before the migration gained momentum. Encouraged by their relative ease of movement, Gawolbe and his mounted horsemen zigzagged across the grassfields with no clear aim in mind, except perhaps to go on — and on.

Bafreng was their first known victim. They ransacked it, breaking up the settlement into three groups — one followed Chief Ngufor I into asylum in Bikom, another fled to Bafut and a third took refuge in Babadju. From Bafreng, the Chamba ravaged Bambui and harassed Bafut.[25] Gawolbe then raided as far west as Ngie, where he put up his headquarters.[26]

It was while at Ngie that the first split in the alliance occurred. Fissures had begun to appear, eroding Gawolbe's authority. Then Gyando broke away, taking his own people northwards through Wum to Takum where they settled. It was a parting of ways that resulted from a serious misunderstanding, because the two Chamba leaders both vacated Ngie and went in opposite directions. Gawolbe turned south and raided through Meta country until he reached the village of Bamunyi at the edge of the forest. And here he paused, to contemplate the future ahead of him.

Not much remained of that future. The long migration had taken

---

24   J.P. Warnier, op. cit., p. 299.
25   Pat Ritzenthaler, *The Fon of Bafut*, (London: Cassel, 1966), p. 30.
26   Kaberry and Chilver, op. cit., p. 17.

a heavy toll on him: he was an old man now, weary of travel and exhausted by the pressures of war and leadership. And yet he seemed to see no end to the migration.

Gazing at the frowning forest, Gawolbe was perplexed. He had never seen anything so intimidating. Wondering what lay beyond, he pondered whether to venture into the mysterious unknown or turn back unto familiar ground and lived experience. That was the question that troubled his mind as he stood before the dark tropical forest, several years and hundreds of miles away from the open fields of the Faro-Deo, knowing that he did not have all eternity to think about it.

TWO

Break-Up of the Chamba Alliance

Gawolbe did not need long to make up his mind. With age, his passion for adventure had diminished. Moreover, mounted men like the Chamba were clearly ill-at-ease in any environment that impaired their vision.

Encounter with the Forest and the Swing Eastwards

According to Bali traditions recorded by I.F. Pefok, the stay at Bamunyi lasted several months as Gawolbe matured his decision about the future.[1] To balance his judgement, he dispatched one of his generals, Gabana, supported by the bulk of the Chamba cavalry, to venture south and report on the prospects of the forest.

As they awaited his return, it became clear that Bamunyi could not support the Chamba for a long time. It was a very small village, with little loot to offer. Even the food available was not suitable: the Chamba were voracious consumers of grain, who now found themselves in a land of tubers! The absence of an appropriate diet suddenly became a potential danger to the visitors.

And as if that was not enough, a very grim message came through from Gabana. The venture south had failed. In spite of successful early raids against Tinto and Tali, the majestic tropical forest finally overwhelmed them. It stood defiantly still, swallowing everything that came at it. Then it unleashed swarms of venomous insects, probably tsetse flies, which attacked the horses, injuring many and killing some.

1   I.F. Pefok, op. cit., p. 2

Gabana was forced to retreat towards Fontem, from where he sent word to Gawolbe to call off the adventure. The forest was not only unhealthy; it was clearly unsuited to their tactics.

Gawolbe made up his mind instantly. The loss of so many of the horses was a crippling blow. He decided to return "home." But first he had to link up with Gabana at Fontem. It was a cruel irony that the Chamba who lived by harassing others should be brought down by an enemy from whom they did not wish to take anything. Still, it was nothing to be ashamed of; with time, the tropical forest would defeat anybody!

The Battle of Kolm and the Death of Gawolbe

The harrowing tales of Gabana's expedition made Gawolbe impatient to leave Fontem. The Chamba skirted the precipitous slopes and came to a place called Bafou-Fondong, on the Chang plateau.

The soothing freshness of the plateau aroused the old tiger in Gawolbe: without thinking twice, he launched a fierce attack on Bafou-Fondong, an attack that was to become a turning point in the history of the Chamba alliance.

The cause of the battle is not clear. Some Bali traditions suggest that Gawolbe wanted to unseat the people and settle on their land. He might indeed have been attracted by the lushness of the plateau and its abundance in grain. But the Chang plateau, being only two days' march from Fontem could hardly be an ideal home for a people fleeing from the forest. It is more probable that the battle of Bafou-Fondong was one of the routine engagements of the warmongers of the alliance, designed to restore their shaken confidence.

Indeed, the war might have been a stereotype Chamba invasion, had there not been a few vital changes of circumstance that would profoundly alter its course. Gawolbe's ability to charge at the enemy, which was one of his great strengths, had been seriously diminished by the loss of many of his horses. But most importantly perhaps, there was not the usual element of surprise which gave his raids such a cutting edge. His reputation had preceded him, and the people of Bafou-Fondong were in readiness for him. They had even sought reinforcements from their neighbours, so that Gawolbe's invasion of the little chiefdom of Bafou-Fondong was met by a formidable Bamileke alliance that was in place before the Chamba arrived.

The sole battle was fought at a place called Kumyidla or Kolm, outside Bafou-Fondong, sometime between 1830 and 1835. The battle is remembered for its ferocity. The Chamba came charging in with bow and arrow; but the Bamileke stood their ground, responding with a defiant burst of dane gunfire that surprised the invaders and forced them to retreat.[2] They regrouped and attacked again, and again the Bamileke riposted. Then the Chamba cracked. They had not expected such fierce resistance. They had never experienced protracted warfare. And with their confidence having recently taken a hit from the forest, they panicked -- and dispersed.

The rout of the Chamba has been attributed to what was undoubtedly the most significant casualty of the campaign -- Gawolbe himself. The Chamba hero-leader, like most of his kind, who led from the front, is thought to have fallen in rather controversial circumstances: it is believed by some that he was fatally wounded during the second wave of enemy fire, by others that he was captured and later beheaded, and by some others that he simply and mysteriously "went" away. Whatever the case, his passing spelled instant disaster for the Chamba alliance. Having lost their centre of direction, they retreated from Kolm in total confusion. It was a vicious irony that Gawolbe who had survived many fierce battles in the past should lose his life from attacking such a small enemy. But great men sometimes fall in remote places. And the popular Chamba saying about the tiger who broke his finger in the burrow of a cricket became ominously prophetic.

Gawolbe's death threw the Chamba alliance into disarray. His passing left a huge vacuum of physical leadership and moral direction. As a moving army, the alliance had not taken time to work out a viable system of internal administration. Indeed, everything revolved around Gawolbe, who personified the alliance as supreme military commander, governor and chief priest, all at once. There was no constituted office of deputy to him and no clear-cut provisions for his

2   Interview with the Elders of Bali Gasho, 13 August 1984.

own succession. In times of war -- and the alliance spent most of its time fighting wars -- this acute concentration of power seemed understandable, even desirable, since the war effort, to which everything else was subordinate, had to be directed by a leader in complete control and with a total vision of things. But this system, effective in the short run, underestimated the hazards of war itself. The sudden death of their leader was one of such hazards. It took the alliance into unknown territory: no provisions had been made for the post-Gawolbe era; the Chamba had no experience of replacing a leader in wartime; and Gawolbe had neither groomed an heir nor left a will about his succession. The absence of a will and of any clear favourite led to the explosion of the alliance as rival princes vied for the open succession.

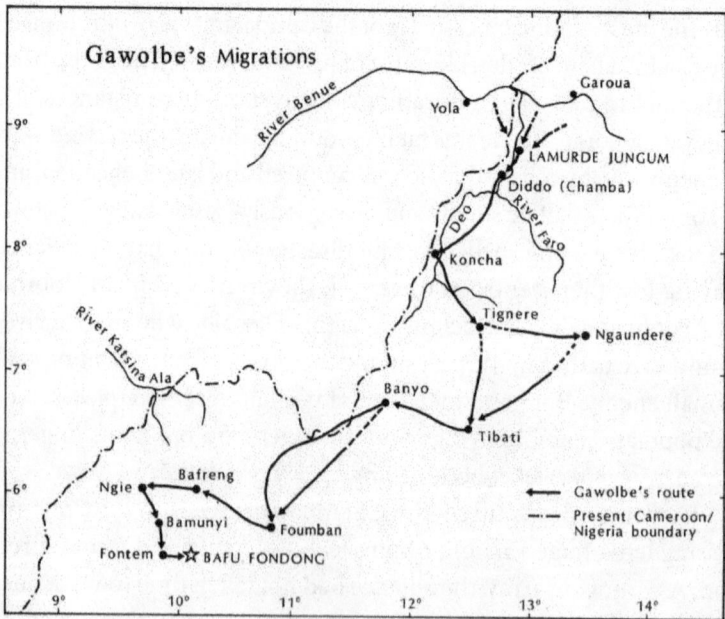

Figure 2.1 Gawolbe's Migrations

Separation

The sequence of events that followed Gawolbe's death is somewhat confusing. It is believed that there was a serious disagreement among the princes over the succession and that the alliance broke up because each prince, unwilling to yield to another, went his separate way with his own supporters.

The venue of the split is a matter of some controversy, with oral traditions in disagreement. There are two contrasting views: the first suggests that the alliance broke up immediately after the battle of Kolm, in the vicinity of Bafou-Fondong itself. But a second view contends that following the disaster of Gawolbe's untimely death, the whole alliance drifted some fifty miles north of Bafou-Fondong to one of three locations where they quarrelled over his succession and split: Waja, near Santa, according to Bali Nyonga traditions;[3] Bagam, according to Bafou-Fondong traditions;[4] and Goksela, near Bagam, according to Bali Gham traditions.[5] This view, although supported by many oral traditions, says nothing about how and by whom the retreat from Bafou-Fondong was organised and directed, even though it is fairly certain that such a retreat could hardly have been a spontaneous drift. In view of the chaos which characterised their departure from Kolm and of the tearful disagreement that was brewing up in their ranks, it is doubtful that the Chamba alliance could have engaged in an orderly fifty-mile retreat, apparently without a recognised leader. Besides, there seems to be no practical reason why they had to wander to the neighbourhood of Santa or Bagam before choosing a leader. It seems more plausible that in the panic, they retreated to their base beyond the battlefield to sort themselves out when disagreement plunged the alliance into a crisis.

This disagreement is one aspect of their history about which the Bali Chamba least agree, as each chiefdom seeks to portray itself as the rightful successor of Gawolbe's kingdom and to shift the blame for the ensuing break-up onto others. It is not clear how the disagreement itself originated. It seems that at first there were only two princes competing for Gawolbe's succession -- Samsu and Galanga. At different stages in the dispute, it appears that either had been enthroned, only

3   M.D.W. Jeffreys, op. cit., p. 190.
4   E.M. Chilver, op. cit., p. 45.
5   Ibid.

to face rebellion from the supporters of the other. One version of the story holds that Gawolbe's eldest son, Samsu, was actually enthroned as Gavabe. But the other princes revolted because he was known to be rather weak and tight-fisted. The rebellious princes supported Galanga, Samsu's cadet brother, who was then enthroned. However, Samsu rebelled in turn, refusing to submit to Galanga's authority and, in anger, took his supporters away in a move that precipitated the disintegration of the alliance.[6] Another version attributes the quarrel to a disagreement with their own tradition. According to this version, succession among the Chamba was usually reserved for children begotten through normal deliveries. The version claims that Samsu had been a breech birth, which was regarded as abnormal and consequently disqualified him from the succession. The dispute arose when Samsu denounced this tradition and put himself in contention. Feeling robbed of the throne by the king-makers who invested Galanga instead, the aggrieved Samsu broke away and founded his own kingdom.[7]

It is remarkable how swiftly the alliance disintegrated following the disagreement. It is even more remarkable that no attempts were made to reconcile the feuding princes and unite the kingdom. And the alliance did not just split between the two rival princes. Instead, the dispute brought other candidates into contention, creating an almost free-for-all. The union was written off as every prince capable of mustering a following set off to found his own chiefdom. It was as though they had been looking for an opportunity to fulfil their ambitions of independent leadership. The Samsu-Galanga wrangle provided such an opportunity.

These ambitions were not exclusive to Gawolbe's princes, however. Amid the confusion, one of his princesses did actually try her hand at state-formation -- with remarkable success as we shall see. It also seems that Gawolbe's death put paid to the alliance with the Pyeri or Peli, another branch of the Chamba who had campaigned together

6   Interview with Doh Tangsin and the Elders of Bali Kumbat, 14 August 1984.
7   Interview with M S T Galabe II and the Elders of Bali Gham, 15 August 1984. View supported by Doh Gashu II and Elders of Bali Gasho in interview on 13 August 1984.

with the Ndagambila. Modi, the Peli leader, led them off to establish themselves on their own, as Bali Muti in present-day Nigeria. It is interesting to note, however, that the example of Modi was not followed by any of the Bà'nì or Bǎnten groups. It is perhaps an illustration of the extent to which they had been integrated that they did not survive the crisis as single groups but rather as parts of the new chiefdoms.

In all, six or seven new chiefdoms emerged from the break-up of Gawolbe's roving alliance. Some were named after their rulers or founders, and others by description of their eventual settlements; but all had the common denominator "Bali" prefixing their names as a symbol of their historical unity. As we have seen, Gawolbe's eldest son, Samsu, taking the regnal name of Gavabe, founded the chiefdom of Bali Gangsin. His junior brother, Galanga, settled near Bagam and his chiefdom was accordingly called Bali Bagam or Bali Gham. A third prince, Ganyam, founded a chiefdom later named Bali Gasho after his successor; while a fourth, Galabe established Bali Kumbat. As for the princess, Nahnyonga, she created a kingdom called Bali Nyonga, in favour of her son, Nyongpasi, who reigned as Fonyonga. To these five chiefdoms established by Gawolbe's offspring is to be added a sixth, Bali Muti, founded by the Peli, Modi, who took the title of GaMuti; and a seventh, Bali Konntan, which is regarded by some as a splinter from Bali Muti, perhaps because it was also Peli, and by many as having broken off independently from the source under a leader called Nyemungan who later proclaimed himself as GaKonntan.[8]

Gawolbe's mobile alliance thus exploded into a number of small and sometimes negligible chiefdoms. The battle of Kolm was a watershed in the history of the Chamba. It marked the end of the territorial unity of the alliance, although their cultural identity remained largely intact. It also signalled the end of the aimless wanderings that they had embarked upon since leaving the Faro-Deo, as the search for permanent homes began. The death of Gawolbe introduced an urgency for stable settlement that would have surprised the early campaigners. Before Kolm, they had been given to migration for its own sake,

8   P.M. Kaberry, *Fieldnotes on Bali Nyonga*, 1960, Ms, p. 97.

extracting their livelihood from the areas they raided. Depleted sources were never renewed, since no settlement was envisaged. Further expansion depended on the availability of fresh, unravaged areas. It was a lifestyle that would, in the long run, be undermined by its own logic: as the number of migrant groups increased, the areas to raid inevitably diminished. Which was why after Kolm, each group set out to secure a fixed territorial base, which it staunchly defended against other invaders. The long search for peace and harmony was underway.

THREE

The Emergence of Bali Nyonga

The creation of Bali Nyonga was a serious departure from Chamba norms. Chamba society was an essentially male-chauvinist society, in which the women were unashamedly restricted to household roles. They had nothing to do with public office and were not allowed to entertain political opinion of any kind. So, it came as a shock to the establishment when Gawolbe's daughter, Nahnyonga, joined the club of nation-building princes to found her own kingdom. Under normal circumstances that would have caused a stir. But the Chamba had been so severely shaken by recent events that her bold challenge passed unnoticed.

Nor was the emergence of Bali Nyonga the sole surprise in the break-up of Gawolbe's alliance. Even more surprising was the fact that Bali Nyonga attracted more followers than the other Balis put together. This owed much to Nahnyonga's personal qualities. Although as a popular princess, she belonged to the high Chamba society, she nevertheless succeeded in broadening the circle of her friends to include many from all levels of the alliance. She was so gentle and kind-hearted that she accumulated an impressive capital of sympathy. She spoke softly – and was listened to.

And she was modest and realistic. She made no claim to sit on the throne herself. Instead, she yielded to her son, Nyongpasi, a soldier of renown, who took the regnal name of Fonyonga I. To many, Nyongpasi offered an acceptable compromise to the feuding princes of Gawolbe. He was clearly royal, albeit maternally, and he had ample gifts of charisma, which gave hope to a people in crisis. No wonder, Bali Nyonga was easily the largest of all the Bali chiefdoms.

Although the limelight of Bali Nyonga quickly settled on the person of Fonyonga I, Nahnyonga's prominent role in the making of the new kingdom was immortalised by the creation of the largely ceremonial but nonetheless powerful office of "Màmfòn" or queen mother for her. Popularly referred to as "Kah" (Kǎ) or grandmother, the office became a permanent institution in the kingdom, with its incumbent generally regarded as an important dignitary, whose advice was sought on many matters of state. The creation of that office was not only an act of gratitude from a thankful son; it was a manifestation of the power-sharing that would win Fonyonga many friends. In fact, although he carefully retained the essence of power, he generously involved others in the execution of his plans. In so doing, he cultivated a popular sense of participation in the affairs of the kingdom and created an internal dynamism that was to be one of its main sources of strength. But the neighbourhood of Bafou-Fondong was not a conducive environment for that dynamism to blossom. As the scene of the trauma that dislocated the Chamba alliance, succeeding Bali groups could not afford to hang around. So when last-ditch efforts to hold the alliance together predictably failed, Fonyonga also left, taking the Bali Nyonga on an independent wave of migrations.

The Bali-BaTi Alliance

While the other Bali groups headed in the direction of the Bamenda grassfields, Fonyonga led his people on a north-easterly course, through Bamilekeland and across the river Noun into Bamun territory. They stopped just short of Fumban itself, at a place variously called Tsen or Kuti or Kubale, where they were warmly received by the local inhabitants, the BaTi, and invited to stay. It was an invitation that Fonyonga could hardly refuse, after months of wandering through hostile territory.

The warmth of the BaTi welcome has been diversely interpreted. It has been suggested that they were looking for allies to strengthen their hand in the running conflict with the Bamun. But it is to be remembered, however, that the BaTi of Kuti were the kith and kin of the BaTi who had earlier joined Gawolbe [referred to as Ti-Gawolbe] and most of whom were within Fonyonga's chiefdom. Their return to Kuti, with their old and new friends, was like a return from the diaspora, and a befitting welcome was laid out for them.

But if the stop had been intended to be temporary, the reception of the BaTi convinced Fonyonga to stay. His people began to acquire vast lands on which to settle and farm, gradually spreading their roots as far out as Fochieya, Mbankouop and Nkoumelap on the eastern banks of the Noun.[1] With BaTi support, Fonyonga also consolidated his army and began a series of extensive raids southwards through Bafoussam to Bansoa and Bangante.[2] His successes on these raids prompted Fonyonga to begin to see himself as the alternative power to the Bamun chief. The ensuing rivalry would only be settled on the field of battle.

Contact with the BaTi also had a profound cultural impact on the Bali Nyonga. These latter shed their language, Mubako, and adopted a simplified form of BaTi called Mungaka, a semi-Bantu language of the Mbam-Nkam group of grassfields languages,[3] as their lingua franca.

The circumstances under which Mungaka became the common language of Bali Nyonga has attracted a number of hypothetical explanations, the most plausible being that offered by M.D.W. Jeffreys. He proposes a scenario of two totally unrelated events which were accidentally responsible for the adoption of Mungaka by Bali Nyonga. First, after the battle of Kolm most of the womenfolk of the Chamba alliance followed Bali Muti, whose leader had looked after them during the war, leaving the other Bali short of women. And secondly, constant Bamun raids had severely depleted BaTi of their menfolk. Consequently, "a large number of mateless Bali Nyonga men met a large number of mateless BaTi women" with whom they intermarried. The offspring of those marriages, learning first their mother's tongue, tended to perpetuate Mungaka, to the detriment of Mubako, as the language of Bali Nyonga.[4]

1   Sultan Njoya, *Histoire et Coutume Bamoun*, Memoires de l'IFAN, Centre du Cameroun, 1972, p. 27.
2   E.M. Chilver, op. cit., pp. 52-53.
3   W.E. Hunt, *An Assessment Report on the Bali Clan in the Bamenda Division of Cameroons Province*, Bamenda, 1925, para. 8.
4   M.D.W. Jeffreys, op. cit., pp. 175-176.

With their new language, Fonyonga streamlined his ambitions going forward. One of those was to replace the Bamun as the dominant power in the region, an ambition that developed into a real obsession. He threw caution to the wind and went flat out to achieve it.

The Bali-Bamun War, 1855

Fonyonga warmed up for the ultimate confrontation with the Bamun by raiding the smaller Bamileke chiefdoms. He overcame Bafoussam, Bangante, Banjun and Bansoa, establishing his power over them. That relationship lasted well after Fonyonga himself, when the chiefs of those villages continued to pay homage to the Fon of Bali Nyonga by greeting him with palm wine.[5]

Having thus sharpened his skills, Fonyonga engaged the battle-hardened Mbuombuo in Fumban. The expedition of 1855 scored a dramatic initial victory that surprised Fonyonga himself. Vastly outnumbered and caught completely off guard, Mbuombuo's men fled at the first volley of gunfire, leaving Fumban at Fonyonga's mercy. The Bali chief could hardly believe his luck. But instead of pressing home his sudden advantage, he mysteriously returned to Kuti to savour his victory and draw up new plans. That was a tragic mistake. The unexpected retreat enabled Mbuombuo to recover his composure. He did not wait for Fonyonga to return.

Mbuombuo launched a vicious and perfectly timed counter-attack against the Bali Nyonga at Kuti. His scouts had reported a lapse of concentration in the Bali camp as they went about their farming chores. He pounced on Kuti in a swift and decisive blow. The Bamun left nothing to chance. They had the same advantage of surprise that the Bali had had during the first encounter. But they did not make Fonyonga's mistake. Instead, they pressed their advantage as far as it could go.

The Bali Nyonga offered a resistance of sorts, holding out for most of their men to return from their farms and for hastily summoned help

5   Ibid., p. 176.

from Bali Kumbat. But neither arrived in time to make any sensible impact on the course of the engagement. By the third day of fighting the Bali Nyonga, staring defeat in the face, resorted to a vigorous rearguard action while their women and children sought refuge across the Noun. It was only a matter of time before Mbuombuo laid bare the town of Kuti and pursued the retreating Bali Nyonga until they were well beyond sight.

Fonyonga's confrontation with Mbuombuo had attracted many sympathisers from neighbouring groups, disaffected by constant Bamun harassment. Many followed him from Kuti, further diversifying and strengthening his army. They had no choice but to follow him: having shown open sympathy for Fonyonga, they could not afford to remain in Mbuombuo's neighbourhood. So, Bali Nyonga received a new influx of Bănten from southern Bamun. Like the BaTi, these were mainly remnants of groups that had earlier joined Gawolbe. They fell into two groups: there were those who actually fought alongside Fonyonga, and there were those who did not join the fight but who approved of the action as a means of ridding themselves of Mbuombuo. Among the first group were the Lap, Munyam and Fuleng who took active part in the attack on Fumban to avenge previous defeat by Mbuombuo.[6] The Kundem or Bandem joined on the scene of the battle itself. They were in Fumban in search of six runaway royal wives when Fonyonga attacked. Their chief, Fongwe, gave orders for his men to join forces with the Bali Nyonga against Mbuombuo whom he accused of plotting the escape of his wives.[7] The alliance continued later on when things went sour. The smaller groups which joined the war morally also took Fonyonga's defeat as their own and followed him across the Noun. They included the Dip, Ndiyang, Set, Sangaam, Won, and Nggod, and they were urged on by the Kwen flute dance, "Kumpi."[8]

---

6   E.M. Chilver, op. cit., p. 85.
7   Ibid., pp. 77-78.
8   Ibid., pp. 73-86.

Fonyonga's Reforms

The injection of so much new blood into the Bali Nyonga confederacy called for a substantial reform of its administrative and military structures. The process of reform began long before the Bamun war and continued with even more urgency thereafter. It was greatly helped by Fonyonga's ingenuity and the almost unlimited amount of patronage at his disposal. Some of the beneficiaries of his patronage were personal rewards: like when he spotted the alert smartness of the BaNggod leader and appointed him to head the intelligence unit of the Bali Nyonga army. Or when he gave the BaTi leader, Bangu, charge of the royal medicines.

But the majority of changes introduced were institutional reforms and innovations, aimed at shaping and strengthening the chiefdom. He reformed the system of retainerdom, which had been an exclusive Ndagambila cult, making it possible for people from all groups to volunteer their services to the corps. Palace retainers or "chĭntèd" as they were called thus became an elaborate body that brought the palace closer to the people and increased their personal stake in the future of the chiefdom.

Perhaps the most significant of Fonyonga's innovations was the creation of two consultative and advisory bodies, which assisted him in the daily administration of the chiefdom and sat in quasi-permanent session at the palace in times of crisis. The first of those was the office of sub-chief or chieflet called mfòntə̀' (plural: fòntə̀') and the second was that of privy councillor called "ŋkɔmmfòn" (plural: kɔmmfòn).

The fòntə̀' were generally men of dignity who were either appointed by Fonyonga at the head of allied groups, their proper chiefs having been deposed in war, or as the rightful chiefs themselves, confirmed in office after surrendering gracefully to Fonyonga. This exercise consolidated Fonyonga's paramountcy in the alliance. The title fòntə̀' itself is of Bamileke or Bamun origin, used to refer to conquered chiefs who were stripped of their administrative powers but maintained as symbols of their respective groups. As a fine diplomat, Fonyonga treated his fòntə̀' with respect and etiquette. He nominally shared his power with them and involved them in the running of the chiefdom. His public pronouncements were always prefaced by the statement:

"I and my fòntə̀'...", to emphasize the collective responsibility of the decision to be announced [even when, as usually happened, Fonyonga had made the decision all by himself!].

No wonder the appointment of fòntə̀' was made so judiciously and taken so seriously. Unpopular chiefs were summarily deposed in favour of popular appointees. But with the Buti, the quest for popularity landed Fonyonga in a predicament: two candidates split the allegiance of the group right down the middle. Fonyonga could not antagonise both of them and alienate the group by appointing a neutral person, neither could he split the group by appointing one over the other. He appointed them both as fòntə̀'! In this matter, Fonyonga's discretion was almost without limit. So, while appointing two fòntə̀' for the Buti group alone, he did not feel obliged to appoint one for every group of the alliance. He was satisfied that the very small groups or even big ones that presented no obvious candidates did not need any mfòntə̀'. In all, twelve fòntə̀' titles were created, four among the Bà'nì groups, who were known as fòntə̀'-Bà'nì and eight among the Bănten known as fòntə̀'-Bănten. The fòntə̀'-Bà'nì included: Fomenjeng [Buti], Fokemban [Buti], Fotikali [Tikali], and Foti or Bangu [Ti]; while the fòntə̀'-Bănten included Fokundem, Fongod, Fowon, Fosang, Fosangam, Fofuleng, Foset, and Fomunyam. Other groups such as Kufad among the Bà'nì or Ndiyang, Dip, Lap and Kwen among the Bănten did not have any fòntə̀'. But the door was not shut on them because Fonyonga reserved the right to appoint as many more fòntə̀' as he desired, a ploy that kept all the groups on their toes.

Unlike the fòntə̀', the kommfòn titles were drawn from more restricted circles. As his confidential advisers, he was inclined to appoint either personal friends or other men on whose judgement he could rely. That is why he went to the original Bà'nì alliance for men with tested loyalty. They were seven in number: Tita Kuna [Peli], Tita Gwandiku [Buti], Gwanchelleng [Buti], Gwaabe [Buti], Gwananji [Tikali], Gwayebit [Tikali] and Gwandi [Kufad]. It is noteworthy that the Buti, as the largest contingent of the adherents, received the lion's share of appointments, although Fonyonga reserved the right to create more offices, as a way of rewarding distinguished service to the state.

Those early appointments were peculiar for the astonishing

absence of titleholders from the original Chamba or Ndagambila. Apart from the Peli, Tita Kuna, there was not a single Chamba among the fòntə̀' or kɔmmfòn. This strange omission was understandable nonetheless: the brutal lessons of Bafou-Fondong were still too fresh for Fonyonga to take any chances with the Chamba. Besides, he wanted to be seen to be welding the alliance together by involving the constituent groups in his action, rather than simply extending the overlordship of the original Chamba core.

The administrative reforms were complemented by a reorganisation of the military apparatus. In Gawolbe's time, the army of the alliance had been composed of two sectors: the personal following of the Fon called bĕdmfòn, consisting of the corps of original Chamba warriors, and the tribal regiments of the affiliated leaders vaguely referred to as fòntə̀'. While maintaining the bĕdmfòn, Fonyonga reorganised the fòntə̀' into a number of military lodges called "Manjɔ̀ŋ" under the leadership of the respective sub-chiefs. The Bali Nyonga army thus became a truly confederal army with Fonyonga himself as supreme commander. He also created a War Council to assist him define military policy and coordinate the activities of various sections of the army. The council of eleven, composed of the four fòntə̆'-Bằnì and the seven Kɔmmfòn [it was later increased to twelve when Bali Konntan was absorbed and its leader admitted into the group], regularly met at the palace to deliberate on military tactics and advise Fonyonga on matters of war and peace.

All these changes profoundly transformed and strengthened Bali Nyonga society. By a tactful blend of persuasion and coercion, Fonyonga succeeded in welding together into one self-reliant community, diverse groups, many of which had only come together in the transient adversity of warfare. His greatest strength remained one of his first — his ability to share. The success of his enterprise derived mainly from his willingness to involve every group in the life and fate of the alliance. The result was that the traditions of the new Bali Nyonga became a mixture of the traditions of its component peoples. It was largely to Fonyonga's credit that this new creature had any cultural shape at all. But most astonishing perhaps, was the fact that Fonyonga's power emerged from the process of reform strengthened rather than weakened. By taking the initiative for change, he had converted himself into the spiritual centre of the alliance and the source of power and favour. As the reforms took root, general confidence in his judgement grew, and his charisma ensured popular approval of all his decisions. So, when he decided that he had had enough of the cut-throat rivalry with the Bamun and that the future of the alliance lay further afield, few dissenting voices were raised.

Bali Nyonga in the Bamenda Grassfields

It is not known what attracted Fonyonga to the Bamenda grass-fields. It is possible that news of the settlement of the other Balis in the region had something to do with it. But with Mbuombuo breathing down his neck, crossing the Noun was the only way forward. Having done so, the Bali Nyonga encamped briefly in the Bagam plain where they met and incorporated the Nggonlan, a small group that had been brought from Banggola by a man called Nggela.[9] Then they all moved westward, under pressure from Bali Kumbat who were busy consolidating their influence in the Bagam and Ndop plains.

They stopped at either Bambui,[10] or Bambili,[11] where they staged their annual "Lela" festival. And being a highly traditional people, it is not impossible that they might have stopped just so as to stage the festival and perform its purifying rites. This is all the more probable because they moved on soon afterwards. Or maybe the mock fighting which constitutes the military ritual of the festival raised their appetite for the real thing. They descended upon Bafreng, razing the village, as its inhabitants fled to Bafut and Bikom.[12] They stayed there for about seven years, first on their own and then together with the Bafreng whom they had invited to return from exile.

The return of Bafreng to share the same settlement with Bali Nyonga was a peculiar development. But the astute Fonyonga I had made all his calculations before inviting them back. First, he foresaw

---

9   Ibid., pp. 72-73.
10   Ibid., pp. 72-73.
11   M.D.W. Jeffreys, op. cit., p. 183.
12   Ibid., p. 191.

trouble within the neighbourhood if he had to expand his territorial base. Secondly, it was becoming inevitable that he would have to take on Bali Kumbat. So, he began to organise potential allies. His evaluation of the characteristic strengths and weaknesses of neighbouring groups and the web of their external relations convinced him that the Bafreng were by far the most suitable ally. For a start they were among the finest blacksmiths in the area, a skill so vital to weaponry that Fonyonga would rather compose with it than contend with it. Furthermore, they were visibly nonaligned with the other major groups, a fact confirmed when no one came to their aid during Fonyonga's attack. So he sent emissaries to Bafut and Bikom to invite them back. They had never been comfortable as refugees, and they readily accepted to return to their ancestral home. They became Fonyonga's first allies in the Bamenda grassfields.

Final Settlement

Fonyonga was still settling into his new alliance with Bafreng when he was approached by a certain Tchu'ako from Kunyang in Bali Konntan, with a very interesting offer. The Bali Nyonga were invited to a new settlement, bigger and better than the tight surroundings of Bafreng, one with ample possibilities for expansion. All of it at the modest price of a small war against the Konntan, in which Fonyonga was assured of the support of the Kunyang and their friends. Fonyonga was certain of victory because, as Tchu'ako further revealed, the Konntan were actually short of gunpowder, having depleted their stocks during a recent death celebration.[13]

This was typical of Tchu'ako. It was he who, in bitterness at losing the succession to the Meta chiefdom of Baforchu, had broken away and allied himself with the Bali Konntan against neighbouring Meta villages. And now with news of a more powerful Bali group next door in Bafreng, he deserted the Konntan for the stronger and more numerous newcomers. It is not known whether Fonyonga spotted the renegade in Tchu'ako or just chose to ignore it. But the proposal was

13   E.M. Chilver, op. cit., pp. 73-74.

very interesting indeed, and it could not have come at a better time. The Bali Nyonga were beginning to feel uncomfortable in the exiguous surroundings of Bafreng. The Tchu'ako plan not only promised to resolve that problem, but also promised to resurrect Fonyonga's cherished dream of building a vast and powerful chiefdom. Then there was the initial attraction of an easy military victory, a bonus for someone who adored military exploits. This prospect also enchanted the Meta clans conquered by the Bali Konntan. They saw Fonyonga as the redeemer, come to rescue them from the high-handed Konntan. And they warmed themselves in anticipation of the retributive joy of a comprehensive Nyonga victory. Tchu'ako who had devised the plan was no longer a villain.

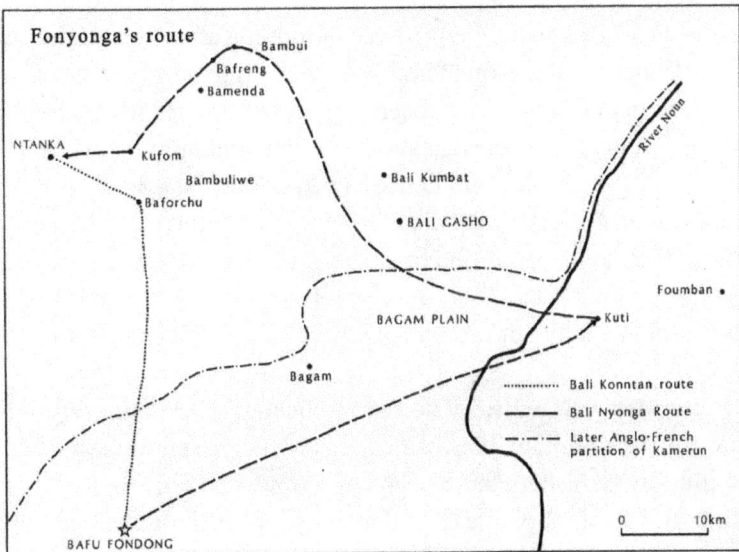

Figure 3.1 Fonyonga's Route

However, the conquest of Bali Konntan turned out to be something of an anti-climax. The Bali Konntan did not offer the type of resistance that would have invited serious fighting. Knowing the overwhelming strength of Bali Nyonga, they made an early peace and with dignity, presented their battle standard, "tutuwàn", to Fonyonga. That flag is still being paraded in Bali Nyonga during the Lela festival. And since both flags were identical, a second red band was added to the Bali Nyonga flag to distinguish it from the Bali Konntan flag.

The Konntan surrender defused the crisis in a way that completely disarmed Fonyonga. Although clearly in defeat, the Bali Konntan seemed to have scored an important moral victory by refusing to fight their Chamba brothers. The result was that Fonyonga did not overrun Fomkonntan. He did not even attack it. Instead, he settled his people on the high ground at a place called Kufom, a few miles east of the Bali Konntan settlement.

But there was no doubting who was the new cock in the yard. From his palace at Kufom, Fonyonga began to send ripples of his authority throughout the land. He took over all the Meta villages that the Konntan had conquered. He rewarded Tchu'ako with the mfòntə' title of Fokunyang and the privilege of looking after the ceremonial horns ("Ntang") of the kingdom.[14] However, his treatment of the Konntan was not as harsh as had been anticipated. In fact, to the dismay of the Meta clans, Fonyonga allowed the Konntan to recover their dignity and even integrate themselves into Bali Nyonga. Their chief was given the title of Fogako and co-opted into the prestigious club of the fòntə'-Bà'nì, a position that made him an automatic member of Fonyonga's War Council. And their "tutuwàn" was not paraded with contempt as a booty of war but alongside the Bali Nyonga "tutuwàn" as a symbol of unity.

The Meta villages felt let down by Fonyonga's conciliatory attitude towards the Konntan. They had expected that these Konntan would be roundly punished and had openly supported Fonyonga to that effect. But it soon became clear that Fonyonga had no desire to fight someone else's war. He was more keen on building Bali Nyonga into a solid kingdom, and he could not begin by alienating any group, least of all a Chamba group.

That exercise began rather badly. An attack on the neighbouring village of Pinyin around the early 1860s went disastrously wrong when the Bali Nyonga, accustomed to fighting in open field, were lured into

14   PM. Kaberry, *Fieldnotes on Bali Nyonga*, 1960, pp. 102-103.

the dense forest between the two villages and comprehensively beaten. Fonyonga was so heartbroken that he never recovered. He died a few months afterwards. He was succeeded by Galega I, who had been born in Banyo around 1820 and had grown up to witness all the triumphs and tribulations of the Chamba alliance. He was well groomed for the succession, having matured in the shadow of the great Fonyonga. As a tribute to the late Fon, Galega decided to avenge the defeat by Pinyin. He knew the magnitude of that defeat, having fought in the battle himself. And, for the same reason, he also knew the terrain around Pinyin, which Fonyonga had not. With a huge force, Galega rounded the forest that had spelled their doom during the first battle, and then walked all over Pinyin.

With the scores level, Galega now turned his attention to the ambitious plan of consolidating the fondom bequeathed by the inventive Fonyonga. He began by making many new friends, notably a large group called Ngiam who, led by one Mbanglin, had left a settlement near Kuti to escape Bamun harassment and followed in Fonyonga's wake to the Bamenda grassfields. They branched off to the neighbourhood of Goksela for a while before returning to the trail of Fonyonga. When the Bali Nyonga settled at Kufom, the Ngiam stopped at a place called Mbafum, outside Bande. And coincidentally, Mbanglin died shortly after Fonyonga, and his successor, Basi, decided to join Galega I. The latter gave him the title of Fongiam and assimilated him to the Fòntǎ'-Bǎnten.[15]

But Galega's task was not all a bed of roses. His reign had its fair share of trials, one of which was an unexpected attack on them by Bali Kumbat around 1864. The attack was the first in a series of fratricidal wars between the two fondoms. And it caused Galega to abandon the settlement at Kufom and join the Konntan in the relatively distant security of Ntanka, which they have occupied ever since.

That shift, though small, took Bali Nyonga even deeper into the Widikum heartland. The new settlement was completely surrounded by Widikum peoples: by Ngemba villages, Moghamo groups, and

15   E.M. Chilver, op. cit., pp. 78-79.

Menemo villages. They had recovered from the upheaval of Gawolbe's passage and now had to contend with the arrival of Bali Nyonga, which further disrupted the tribal composition and cultural balance of the region. The history of Bali Nyonga would thenceforth be dominated by the vicissitudes of its relationship with its neighbours.

From the onset, those relations were bound to be discordant. Galega's settlement was resented by the Meta clans who were pushed out in the process. And by returning to the vicinity of earlier Chamba raids, the Bali Nyonga aroused the ire of the Widikum tribes which had suffered from those raids. Galega's men thus found themselves held to answer for the doings of another Chamba era. Indeed, the cohabitation of Bali Nyonga with the Widikum peoples around it became the most significant element in the geopolitics of the southern Bamenda grassfields.

FOUR

Consolidation of the Fondom

The expansion of the realm of Bali Nyonga was a natural sequel of their settlement. It was carried out with purpose and speed, meeting little resistance because they were much better equipped in arms and experience than any of their opponents. That expansion was the work of Galega I, a larger-than-life figure, with larger-than-life-ambitions.

Galega I came to power under the sort of circumstances that breed legends: Bali Nyonga had just suffered humiliation from Pinyin, and the heart-broken Fonyonga I had died, as if by delayed action. Then Galega arrived, bringing youth and vitality to a weary and languid people.

He began his reign with reassuring certainty. His devastation of Pinyin worked miracles on the morale of his people. But he refused himself any complacency. He was convinced that the destiny of Bali Nyonga as an important kingdom could only be achieved at the price of more sacrifice. He was ready to make that sacrifice, and to summon the same from his people.

Galega launched a vast programme of arms procurement and a sweeping reform of the military structures. Bali Nyonga had always been very well armed for its time and environment. But Galega was a man of superlatives. He entered the arms market with a rousing appetite, stockpiling dane guns and other weapons brought in from the coast and from the north through the Benue River trade routes. The exact size of his arsenal was never published. But the Germans estimated, upon arrival in 1889, that the Bali Nyonga were in possession of at least two thousand dane guns.[1] For a neighbourhood where most villages were fewer than two thousand, all told, that was a formidable force indeed.

Galega turned his attention next to the structure and tactics of his army. The Bali Kumbat invasion which forced him out of Kufom had exposed many of the shortcomings of the Bali Nyonga army. No longer a migrant, offensive army who struck at will and moved on, Bali Nyonga was now a settled force with territory to defend. This new development prompted Galega to increased pragmatism in his approach to warfare.

He had inherited an army composed essentially of two parts: the Fon's personal following or bĕdmfòn and the following of the fòntɔ̀' which Fonyonga I had reorganised into "Manjɔ̀ŋs." Galega I streamlined this organisation still further. He reduced the bĕdmfòn to a select bodyguard of retainers, and then grouped the rest of his personal following into a new lodge called "ndânjì".

The principal shortcoming of the confederal system of "Manjɔ̀ŋs" was that its leadership was somewhat diffused.[2] Which was to be expected because the fòntɔ̀'-Bănten who commanded the "Manjɔ̀ŋs" were not members of the Fon's War Council. The directives of the Council were relayed to them second-hand and got to the soldiers as third hand and sometimes contradictory orders. In warfare, this could spell instant disaster. Galega used this extraordinary situation as excuse for a major shake-up of the whole system. He initiated two main reforms that changed the face of the Bali Nyonga military system. First, he united all the "Manjɔ̀ŋs" into two armies, under the leadership of his two eldest sons — Tita Nji and Tita Gwenjang, whom he co-opted into the War Council. Tita Nji's army, which incorporated the Bà'nì groups, was called "ndanjem," while Tita Gwenjang's army, incorporating the Bănten contingents was referred to as "manded." Within each army, other important princes had lodges of their own: in "ndanjem" Tita Fonja and Tita Lavod had "ndâle" and "Ndâŋgɔ̀'" respectively, while in "manded" Tita Ladinga and Tita Mongu ran

1   Chilver and Kaberry, op. cit., p. 67.
2   Pat Ritzenthaler, *The Fon of Bafut*, (London: Cassel, 1966), para. 2.

"ndâŋkwà'" and "ndamukɔ̀ŋ." Secondly, Galega created a War Assembly of all soldiers taking part in each campaign. The Assembly met in the village green on the eve of the engagement and was briefed by the Fon in person on the decisions of the War Council and the plan of battle. All those reforms tightened Galega's control of the army. He retained direct command of the bĕdmfòn and "ndânjì," which were sometimes deployed independently in limited wars. In case of general mobilisation, however, only the former remained attached to the person of the Fon, while the latter was integrated into one of the armies. And by placing his sons at the head of both armies, Galega ensured that the operational control of the entire military fell firmly under his belt.

Military discipline was reinforced, and the planning of wars made more elaborate. Galega usually consulted lengthily with the War Council and insisted on briefing the War Assembly himself, spelling out the object of the expedition as well as the time and place of assembly. The selection of the assembly point, called "Ntânbèd," was based on ample knowledge of the logistics of the enemy and the surrounding terrain. The march to the "Ntânbèd" generally took place at night, so as to take position in the darkness and prepare for assault in the small hours of the morning. The signal for action was usually fire, which the advance party of scouts called "gwè" would have crept into the village and put on a few houses. At the sight of the flames, the army would charge, raining gunfire and wreaking havoc.

This act was repeated with devastating accuracy over the next few years, as Galega launched assault after assault to subdue neighbouring villages. The sequence of attack is difficult to reconstruct since there was no established plan of action. But the main thrust of attack was the Widikum villages to the west and south-west which "on account of their characteristic lack of cohesion, were quite unable to withstand the Bali attacks."[3]

Bali Nyonga's control over its sphere of influence was not as centralised as the Bamun's. Villages conquered by Galega were usually left

3   C. H. Croasdale, *Intelligence Report on the Bali*, 1932.

in possession of their lands and houses or, if driven out at first, were soon allowed to return. It was his policy not to carry out indiscriminate annexations of territory, with the result that although the influence of Bali spread throughout its realm, Bali Nyonga itself did not grow much bigger. Suzerainty centred around tribute, not physical expansion. Conquered people, who were referred to as "niwɔmbè," the Mubako term for subject people, were bound to pay tribute to the Fon of Bali in the form of farm products, firewood, women, and labourers, plus all royal perquisites such as elephant tusks and leopard skins.

Though compulsory, the tribute had no established timetable or quotas: it could be brought in whatever quantity, at any time and as many times as possible. It was organised and collected on behalf of the Fon by prominent notables and princes called "tǎdmànjì," who served as the Fon's representatives in the conquered villages.

Such then was the legacy that Galega I bequeathed to Tita Gwen-jang [also known as Tita Mbo], who succeeded him as Fonyonga II in 1901. In the twilight of Galega's long reign, there had been a serious scare that his passing might lead to a disastrous fight for the succession, all too painfully reminiscent of Bafou-Fondong, as the old Fon vacil-lated between the two frontrunners — Tita Nji and Tita Gwenjang.[4] Fortunately, disaster was averted when Tita Nji predeceased Galega I in 1896, leaving Tita Gwenjang as the sole candidate for the succession in 1901. Although Tita Lavod did make a half-hearted attempt to present himself as a contender, that challenge was easily seen off and Tita Gwenjang became Fonyonga II to almost unanimous acclaim, inaugurating a reign that was notable as much for what it did as for what it failed to do.

Born at Kufom around 1856, Fonyonga began his reign on an emotional note, by retrieving Gawolbe's remains and instruments from Bafou-Fondong. He had threatened war unless the fallen Chamba

4   Tita Nji's contention for the succession is rather interesting as it contradicts with later Bali tradition that an heir to the throne must have been born from the throne, that is, whilst his father was already Fon. Whereas Tita Nji had been born in Bafreng in the time of Fonyonga I, seven or eight years before Galega I became Fon. It is possible therefore that the tradition was a rather recent development dating perhaps only from Fonyonga II himself.

leader's remains were returned to him. And not knowing what to make of the ultimatum, the chief of Bafou-Fondong surrendered the well-preserved head of Gawolbe, together with his famous double-gong. He also sent an indemnity of three girls and five dane guns. From the onset of his reign, Fonyonga had the dignity of receiving Gawolbe's camwooded head and ceremonial gong, "giligwa," which is today one of the foremost symbols of royal authority in Bali Nyonga. A date was fixed for the proper burial of the retrieved remains. The ceremony brought together, for the first time since Bafou-Fondong, all the Bali Chamba kings, and it lifted a heavy moral burden from their shoulders.

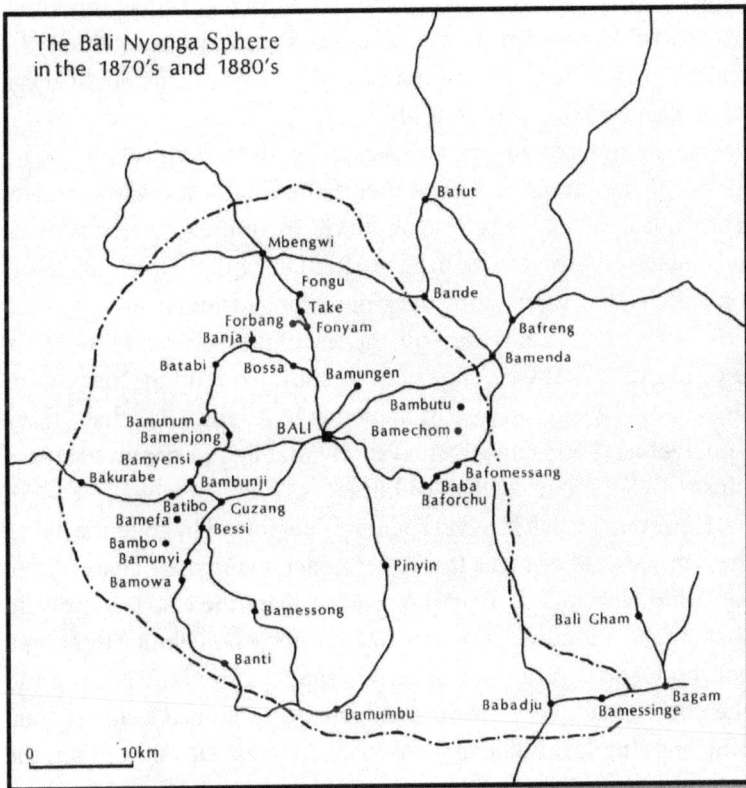

Figure 4.1 The Bali Nyonga Sphere in the 1870s and 1880s

Thanks to Fonyonga II, an important missing link in Chamba

history was restored by an act that put them at peace with themselves and at one with their past. Gawolbe himself would have been pleased with the elaborate celebration of his "return." Fonyonga II was more than pleased with the initiative that had brought it about.

The recovery of Galwobe's remains was the signature achievement in a reign of numberless variations of fate and fortune. For, although Fonyonga II inherited a realm that he had helped forge as commander of "Manded," he came to the throne in rather difficult and uncertain times. The Europeans had come, bringing with them a government that forbade all wars except their own. Fonyonga inherited his father's friendship with the Germans, but he soon discovered that in spite of that friendship he could not expand the realm that he had inherited. A soldier of his brilliance was reduced to the role of maintaining the status quo. But even that was not to be an easy task. The post-Galega years witnessed the birth of Widikum resistance to the status quo, as they began to question the very basis of Bali suzerainty over them. They could not understand how their fathers had allowed themselves to be subjected by Galega. And as the Germans preached tribal peace and equality, many of them began to hesitate with their tribute to the Fon of Bali. They were testing the ground for a major revolt that would rock the realm in later years. Still, the fact of Bali suzerainty could not be contested. Chief Cherenge of Baba summed it up for the records when he told a land inquiry in Bamenda in August 1922 that "There is none of us [Meta chiefs] who can say that he did not give leopard skins to Bali."[5] None challenged him!

However, the Bali Nyonga realm was not forged by conquest alone. They only waged war as a last resort of achieving their goals. When war could be avoided, they were glad to spare the effort. In fine old Chamba tradition they welcomed all groups who voluntarily sought their protection. While at Kufom, Galega I received the Ngiam, and when he moved over to the present site he welcomed a small group of Balengsang from Baleng. Curiously, Meta groups other than the Kunyang also sought Bali Nyonga protection. Notable among them

5   Evidence on the Bali-Baforchu Boundary Dispute, given before Inquiry led by W.E. Hunt, D.O. Bamenda, August 1922.

were the BaMungen [now Ngienmbo] who came to Bali in great distress, as Fombu revealed to an inquiry in Bamenda:

> When we migrated from Widikum, we settled here (in pres-
> ent-day Bali Nyonga). The Bali Konntan came and drove
> us. So we fled to Bamenta (Kominyang). Then the Bamenta
> people started to "put us for pot and chop us plenty." We
> heard that Bali Nyonga had come and conquered the Bali
> Konntan so we returned and clapped hands to the Fon.[6]

Galega I re-settled them in northern Bali.

Fonyonga II continued the policy of swelling Bali ranks by wel-
coming distressed groups. Among his first guests were the Meta chiefs
of Bossa, Mbufung and Mbelu, who followed the example of the
Bamungen and came with their groups to seek Fonyonga's protection.
He settled them in the outskirts of Bali, to the north-west, west and
south respectively. He also received and re-settled in his south-eastern
suburbs, the Baforchu who came in from Mankon where they had
taken refuge in the heat of the first Chamba raids, but from where
they were now expelled for playing instruments on "Kwifon's" day.

Nor were Fonyonga's new adherents all of Widikum origin. There
was, for example, a group of BaTi who arrived from around Bansoa
[now Penka-Michel] in 1904. They were of the same stock as the
Ti-Gawolbe and the BaTi who had received Fonyonga I at Kuti. But
when, under Bamun pressure, Fonyonga abandoned Kuti, taking
the bulk of the BaTi with him, a small contingent remained behind
hoping to brave the Bamun onslaught. They failed, as they were soon
uprooted from Kuti and sent wandering across the Bamileke grassfields. They eventually reached Bansoa, from where they had news
of their relatives in Bali Nyonga and decided to join them. Fonyonga
II welcomed them as old friends and settled them to the south-east
of his heartland. And so the Ti-Mbundam, as they were known in
Bali, in reference to their secondary origin in Bamelike or Mbundam

---

6   Testimony to the Inquiry under the Inter-tribal Boundaries Settlement Ordinance,
    Bamenda, December 1948 - March 1949.

country, ended years of miserable wandering in a new land of peace. They even became landlords as well. Two years after arriving Bali Nyonga, their chief received a distress call from his brother-in-law, the chief of Bawok, and invited him to Bali. Bawok was a little Bamileke village outside Bangante, whose chief, Nana, fell out with his neighbours for showing off his annual dance, "Kam." These neighbours, mainly Bangante, Tongfegha and Bandiangse, who could not match Nana's pomp in their own annual dances, conspired to drive him from the land because, though only a small chief, he was fast becoming the centre of attraction in the neighbourhood. Very reluctantly, Nana left Bawok, taking part of his people with him. He tried to settle at nearby Bangwa-Bangante, but they would not have him. So, Nana sought asylum with his brother-in-law in Bali Nyonga. The Ti-Mbundam chief granted the request and sent envoys to conduct the Bawok to Bali where they were settled at a place called Kumchu, behind the Ti-Mbundam settlement.[7]

The location of these vassal groups is interesting. Rather than disperse them within the kingdom, they were maintained as whole units and settled in a ring-like formation round the core of Bali Nyonga. The disposition served an evident military purpose: in time of war, the cordon of vassal villages formed a protective shield, absorbing the initial shock of any invasion and giving Bali Nyonga valuable time to adjust and react. In normal times they were the watchtowers of the kingdom itself.

Such then was the nature and extent of the Bali Nyonga realm in the mid-nineteenth century. It was the largest of its kind throughout the Bamenda grassfields. And it was also the most varied, consisting of a conglomerate mixture of peoples and groups from different origins, cultures and horizons. Some had campaigned together for so long that they had virtually blended into a homogeneous body. But many were new and strange to the realm, and some would remain culturally irreducible throughout. Indeed, some would even have been at war with one another had it not been for the Bali, and some would soon

---

7   E.M. Chilver, "A Bamileke Community in Bali Nyonga : A Note on the Bawok", *African Studies*, 23, Nos 3-4, 1964.

be at odds with Bali itself.

This extraordinary diversity of history and culture made the governance of Bali Nyonga a very intricate matter indeed, needing a firm hand to bring stability to what looked nearly like a madhouse.

Administration of the Realm

The dominant feature of the Bali Nyonga polity was the immense cult of the ruler. Power was very heavily concentrated in the hands of the Fon. He was the supreme judicial authority, his decisions in that capacity being promptly and ruthlessly enforced by the closed regulatory society called "Ŋgùmba"; he was overlord of the land, and he made final decisions in matters of peace and war. He made appointments to important state offices as he saw fit. He was entitled to the services of the people for both public and private duty: apart from cultivating his farms and building houses for his wives, he expected a non-royal family head to give him a son as a retainer or a daughter in marriage.

Families were eager to render this service because of its potential benefits: retainers were always within earshot of the most important decisions, and royal brides lived within touching distance of becoming the mother of the next king! Either way, the service gave the family concerned a priceless foothold in the palace. The Fon's claim to the services of his people was without limits in time of war when the entire kingdom stood mobilised at his command.

These comprehensive prerogatives derived from the fact that the Fon of Bali was basically a distinguished military leader. The state of Bali had been built from a roving army in which unflinching loyalty to the commander and total dedication to the common cause were essential for the very survival of the state. By the time they found peace and settlement, this act of sheer military discipline had become the basis of their polity. The principle of the Fon's accountability was thus absent. So too was the constituted office of deputy to the Fon, because in Bali military understanding supreme command was unique, not shared. And so, the Fon of Bali, though basically not a divine king, gradually developed many of the trappings of divine monarchy.

Nevertheless, the Fon did delegate some of his powers to appointed ward-heads who settled local problems on his behalf. But when the parties concerned were not satisfied with the ruling of the ward-head, they appealed to the "Kɔm", who constituted the second tier of juris-diction. And if the parties were still not satisfied, then they could be brought before the supreme justice of the Fon himself.

The Fon also had a formal War Council that he consulted and a War Assembly that he informed. When he had other matters of national importance to report to the people, a great council of the realm was summoned, although this was more in the nature of a durbar than a deliberative body. Five groups normally took part in such councils: fòntə̀', kɔm, "chǐntèd," priests of the Vòma cult known as "ŋwàna," and royal princes. But the Fon had a largely free hand in the choice of his advisers and personal attendants. Although he usually consulted various individuals as occasion and preference dictated, he was neither bound to seek their advice nor to accept it when given. And even though most offices were hereditary, the Fon reserved the right to appoint more and to rely on whosoever he wished.

The second feature of the Bali Nyonga polity, which reinforced the first, was the tendency to stress the appointive nature of public office. Again, this was related to the military origins of the state. Military prowess was not hereditary, although there were some very distinguished military families. Consequently, the Fon compensated individual talent and achievement irrespective of kinship. In other words, there was equal opportunity for political and military honour, the emphasis being on talent, not on traditional red tape.

The cult of leadership was also aided by the composition of the chiefdom: the fact that the people were of such diverse origins made it difficult for the emergence of entrenched and legitimate countervailing authorities capable of challenging the Fon. The cult was fostered by the outstanding longevity of the Fons. Galega I reigned for forty-four years, Fonyonga II for thirty-nine. During such long reigns, capable rulers strongly consolidated their position.

Yet, notwithstanding their immense power, Fons of Bali did not become tyrants. This was the third characteristic of the Bali Nyonga polity which, like the others, also had its roots in the kingdom's mil-itary past. For it was common knowledge that an effective military leader had to maintain a certain degree of closeness with his people, based on the common destiny of the battlefield. For their own good as well, the Fons of Bali could not afford to tyrannise their subjects.

This was one of the things that struck the German explorer, Zint-graff, when he arrived Bali in 1889. As he noted in his diary, Galega I "was very clever at sensing the wishes of the populace. Nothing was undertaken and no law was announced without the certainty that it would be carried out."

The leadership cult in Bali Nyonga was strengthened by the benevolence of that leadership. The cult was so powerful that it was considered an outrage to challenge the authority of the Fon. And if this came from within the kingdom itself, it was dealt with summarily, often by banishment. This situation was dramatically demonstrated in a misunderstanding between Fonyonga II and the Ti-Mbundam chief. The friendship between them went drastically sour when the latter began to encroach on the prerogatives of the Fon. Not that the Ti-Mbundam chief had always been a humble guest. In fact, no sooner had he arrived in Bali than he began to think of creating his own independent sphere of influence. In 1906 he invited the hapless Bawok to Bali. Then he began to create his own sub-chiefs, without bothering to refer the matter to the Fon. And as carvers, they offered themselves very imposing stools! Fonyonga was incensed. He promptly withdrew all the raphia bushes that he had given to the Ti-Mbundam and put them under virtual quarantine. In October 1911, as many as 500 of them marched to Bamenda to complain to the Colonial Government about Bali Nyonga oppression. In response, the Divisional Officer personally went to Bali to try to reconcile both parties. But after three weeks of mediation, he conceded failure as both sides remained adamant. So, the Government implemented the only solution possible — all 3000 Ti-Mbundam were physically removed from Bali and re-settled near Bagam. As they left, they captured chief Nana of Bawok who had supported Fonyonga in the dispute. They kept him prisoner until a delegation of retainers, sent by the Fon of Bali and comprising Njimonikam and Dingbula, negotiated his release in 1912. When Nana returned, Fonyonga rewarded his loyalty by settling his people on the land vacated by the Ti-Mbundam.

The Ti-Mbundam crisis was an eye-opener to anyone within the chiefdom who thought he could challenge the authority of the Fon of Bali. But that authority, so tangible in Bali Nyonga proper, was less obvious in the other villages of the realm. This was not all down to physical presence or absence. Rather, the Bali Nyonga style of conquest and expansion was such that the Fon did not allow himself to become embroiled in the administration of subject villages. Galega I was convinced that the most effective way of administering such villages was through their own proper chiefs, so he allowed those chiefs to retain their traditional dignity and administrative responsibility over their people. He treated with the chiefs, who in turn treated with their people, a case of indirect rule par excellence.

Yet Galega's intentions for the realm have remained somewhat enigmatic. He did not assimilate the subject villages. They were not involved in the central administration of the realm. They were not consulted on the formation of alliances or on other matters of war and peace. They had no representatives at any of the councils of state. And they were not part of the Bali regular army, although their services were requisitioned in times of need. In Galega's mind, as in Fonyonga's, the realm existed mainly as a source of personal prestige, of tribute and of labour.

But if the Bali realm was rather diffuse in structure, it was alive nonetheless, with everyone's obligations clearly understood. From the onset there was a gentleman's agreement between the Fon of Bali and the subject chiefs to protect the interests of the realm as a whole and of Bali Nyonga in particular. To see to this, subject villages liaised with the royal court in Bali through intermediaries called "tǎdmànjì".

The "tǎdmànjì" were prominent notables and princes who, though resident in Bali, were the Fon's mouthpiece in the villages and his agents for the collection of tribute and the organisation of labour for public works. The corps varied in size as the sphere of influence expanded. As shown below, the functions of "tǎdmànjì" were concentrated within a select handful of men — only nine of them in the early days of Fonyonga's reign — most of whom were responsible for more than one village at a time.

As an administrative system, the setup of the "tǎdmànjì" was rather peculiar. There was no coordination among them, and they did not constitute a recognised body. Although the office originated in Galega's time, the criteria and mode of selection remained unclear throughout. While some were definitely appointed by the Fon, many simply arrogated the position, becoming answerable to the Fon more out of loyalty than out of duty. Nor were the functions of "tădmànjì" clearly defined. Some maintained the classic role of faithful and loyal middlemen, relating courteously with the subject chiefs and seeing themselves in no other light than that in which the Fon chose to project them. But others interpreted their roles more liberally, reading into the office great opportunities for personal aggrandisement. These were the imperious "tădmànjì" who regarded themselves as the effective rulers of the subject villages, constantly by-passing the local chiefs to deal directly with the people, and often hatching plans in the Fon's name about which the Fon himself had no idea. The most imperious of them all was the awesome Tita Lavod, whose immense figure simply towered over the tributary villages. The story goes that he once had his eye on a charming Batibo princess. But the chief of Batibo, unwilling to part with that particular princess, sent him five others instead. Tita Lavod sold the girls and got his princess!

Table 4.1 Bali Nyonga Tădmànjì in the Mid-19th Century

TĂDMÀNJÌ	VILLAGES CONTROLLED
1. Tita Fofam	Mungen Muwa, Bambunji, Bamunyenji, Foratshu, Fometu, Bakuragbe, Bambu, Batabi
2. Tita Mufut	Besi, Guzang, Bamunyi, Bamefa, Baba
3. Tita Lavod	Batibo and Neighbouring Meta chiefdoms
4. Tita Fokum	Bamunung, Bamenjong, Bamessong, Bamessinge, (previously under Tita Gwenjang)
5. Tita Sikod Foncham	Baforchu, Pinyin, Bangan
6. Tita Ladinga	Bangwa, Bamechom
7. Tita Nji	Bawo
8. Kungwe	Babaju
9. Keninga Tashim	Mungen Mbu

The intrinsic value of the "tădmànjì" system is hard to measure.

While some tributary villages had none at all, the "tǎdmànjì" in some cases spread themselves so thin as to be barely efficient. Tita Fofam had as many as eight villages; Tita Fokum had five, stretching across the width of the realm from Bamenjong to Bamessinge. Yet, however thin the cover in some places, the system of Tǎdmànjì symbolised the hegemony of Bali Nyonga over its tributary villages. It was a system of supervision and surveillance put in place for the supply of tribute and labour.

As Bali Nyonga grew, it also developed into a major commercial centre. It became the main clearing house in a flourishing north-south trading system, with arms, salt and cloth brought in from the coast in exchange for slaves and ivory from further inland. Trading at its weekly market featured goods from several sources, notably: tobacco from Pinyin, iron and leather works from Babungo and Bamessing, groundnuts from Ndop, mats from Bafut, palm products from Meta, mudfish and kola nuts from Baforchu, smoked fish from Bambalang, crayfish from Tiko and clothing from Calabar.

Galega I established trade relations with many other chiefdoms, making his people the most travelled group in the grassfields. Among his new partners were Fumban, previously a sworn enemy, Bafreng, Mendankwe, Bansoa, Babessong, and Babungo.

Bali Nyonga's rise to prominence inevitably led to rivalries with the more established states of the neighbourhood, especially Mankon and Bafut. The competition was all the more bitter because, with the extra attraction of being the newest and most exciting force in the region, Bali Nyonga was gaining the allegiance of chiefdoms that would otherwise have gravitated towards either of the two existing powers. Not only that, Galega I and Fonyonga II after him actively engaged in policies designed to undercut the alliances of rival powers by offering generous terms to returning refugees of earlier Chamba raids and promising trade, friendship and greater freedom to the clients of their rivals. These policies were seen by the other powers as outright subversion.

Owing to its geographical proximity to Bali Nyonga, Mankon was more a target of this practice than Bafut. When Mankon pun-ished Baforchu for desecrating Kwifon's day, Bali Nyonga welcomed them, thereby nullifying the effect of the Mankon sanction. The policy was pursued even more aggressively in the smaller villages of their common neighbourhood: Bamechom [Chomba], Bambutu [Mbatu] and Bangwa [Nsongwa]. Prior to the arrival of Bali Nyonga, Mankon regarded all these villages as falling within its sphere of influence. Then Bali Nyonga poached them into its own sphere of influence, entrenching the Mankon-Bali bitterness still further.

Curiously, however, the most serious rival of Bali Nyonga was not from within the neighbourhood. It came from still another Bali. The intrinsic big-fist attitude of the Bali Chamba made Bali Kumbat an almost natural opposition to Bali Nyonga. The rivalry between them assumed such proportions that it is one of the most controversial chapters of Bali history.

Inter-Bali Rivalries

The idea of conflict between Bali Nyonga and Bali Kumbat is today a source of deep embarrassment to both sides. Yet in the early nineteenth century it was almost a fact of life. By the mid 1860s relations between the two chiefdoms had deteriorated so badly that they had virtually lapsed into a state of perpetual conflict. Three wars were fought between them, one in Bali Kumbat and two in Bali Nyonga, as the initiative changed hands from one to the other. The fortunes of war also changed, although in the final analysis neither side won any conclusive victories.

The immediate causes of the wars varied, sometimes involving rather trifling excuses, but the underlying cause of conflict remained the same — a foreseeable clash of ambitions between them. In the first phase of settlement in the Bamenda grassfields, Bali Kumbat was the most prominent Bali state. But the arrival of Bali Nyonga threatened that prominence. Bali Nyonga actually tried to avoid Bali Kumbat by circling through Bambui to Bafreng and then moving even further away to the far west of the Bamenda grassfields. Yet the simple presence of Bali Nyonga within those grassfields was seen as challenge enough to Bali Kumbat who interpreted it as an intrusion into its sphere of influence. It therefore sought to subdue the newcomers before they were permanently settled.

The First Bali Kumbat-Bali Nyonga War

A series of matrimonial problems provided the pretext for the first war between the two chiefdoms around 1866. First, one of Galega's consorts eloped to a Bali Kumbat prince called Nga. Galega remonstrated to Gagwanyin I for the return of his wife, but Nga refused to surrender the woman. Then, as if by arrangement, one of Gagwanyin's wives called Banmi ran to Galega's court, taking her son Nako with her. Galega gratefully held them both as bargain for his runaway wife. He stuck to his guns when Gagwanyin sent goods for their redemption, confiscating the goods instead. Thereupon, Gagwanyin lost his temper and promptly invaded Bali Nyonga.[8]

The scene of this invasion and the course of the ensuing battle are today a matter of debate. Mankon traditions relate that the attack took place while Bali Nyonga was still at Bafreng and that it was stemmed by a united front of Mankon, Bafreng and Bali Nyonga itself. The Bali Kumbat are said to have been forced back to Bambuliwe where chief Fomukong of Mankon inflicted a severe and final defeat upon them. It was after this invasion, according to these traditions, that Bali Nyonga moved from Bafreng to Kufom.[9]

But this version contains several anachronisms. If the war took place while Bali Nyonga was still at Bafreng, then it must have taken place in the time of Fonyonga I, whose contemporary in Bali Kumbat was Galabe I. Whereas all sides agree that the protagonists in the conflict were Gagwanyin and Galega, not Galabe and Fonyonga!

According to Bali traditions, the raid took place while Bali Nyonga was already at Kufom. The main engagement of the campaign was at a place later named "Ngwa'ndikang." The Bali Nyonga were outmanoeuvred and overwhelmed, and they simply dropped their guns and fled, wherefore the name "Ngwa'ndikang" meaning "abandon gun."[10] It has even been suggested that Galega was captured but later escaped.[11] Still, there was no doubting the extent of the rout: scores dead, hundreds

---

8   M.D.W. Jeffreys, *Traditional Sources*, pp. 296 - 297.
9   Chilver and Kaberry, *Traditional Bamenda*, p. 18.
10   E.M. Chilver, *The Bali Chamba of West Cameroon*, p. 65.
11   M.D.W. Jeffreys, *Tribal Notes*, 1951, Mimeo.

wounded, and hundreds more taken prisoner by Bali Kumbat.[12] As an indication that the reason for the war was different from the announced cause, Banmi and her son were never mentioned again!

The Second Bali Nyonga-Bali Kumbat War

Among the captives of the first war was another of Galega's consorts, and mother of a prominent prince called Ndumu. Her liberation was to be the pretext for the next war. It was an offensive that Galega took over a year to prepare, first moving his palace to the more defendable Ntanka and then equipping and reorganizing his army thoroughly.

But the attack itself, late in 1867, was not altogether a surprise to Gagwanyin. He had anticipated that Bali Nyonga would attempt to rescue the captives of the first war. So when, after a two-day march, they reached a place called Fatfat in the outskirts of Bali Kumbat proper, they were met by a strong Bali Kumbat force led by Tita Fongwa. The ensuing battle was fierce and bloody, leaving deep scars on the countryside. But Fatfat was as far as the Bali Nyonga could go. Tita Fongwa successfully checked their advance and prevented them from reaching the heart of the village. In the end they retreated without liberating any of the captives. Instead, they lost more men, notably the valiant chief of Baaku called Njanji.[13] The second war, like the first, was a major blow for Bali Nyonga.

The Third Bali Kumbat-Bali Nyonga War

Encouraged by his successes in both wars, Gagwanyin now sought to overrun Bali Nyonga completely and establish himself beyond any doubt as the predominant ruler in the Bamenda grassfields. So sure, was he of victory that he chose to lead the attack himself.

But the second attack on Bali Nyonga which took place in late 1868, turned out to be ill-conceived and ill-timed. Bali Nyonga was well-prepared. Their new site was far more difficult to penetrate, so hilly it was easy to lay ambush of all sorts. And in readiness for the war, Galega had enlisted the support of Bafreng with whose leader

12   E.M. Chilver, op. cit., p. 65.
13   Ibid., p. 74.

(Azefor II) he had contracted a treaty of friendship, and of Mankon, an erstwhile enemy who was more concerned by the unchecked expansion of Bali Kumbat.[14] Besides, Galega was not going to allow himself to be defeated on home ground for a second time. The second Bali Kumbat invasion offered him an opportunity to avenge the previous defeat.

He seized the opportunity with both hands. He allowed Gagwanyin's men to penetrate deep into Bali Nyonga, so deep that they were within shooting distance of his palace. Then he sprang the trap: the Bali Nyonga emerged from all sides, encircling the Bali Kumbat and closing in on them in such a way as to wipe them out completely. Seeing the hopelessness of their situation, Gagwanyin gave orders to his men to break ranks and retreat. The desperate Mubako cry, "Nepkolbe payila", was heard repeatedly as they struggled to break the ambush. They succeeded in the end, and Gagwanyin and a handful of his soldiers escaped. But many perished. And the Bali Nyonga promptly renamed the scene of engagement "Payila", after the Bali Kumbat battle cry, in memory of a famous victory.

However, the rivalry between Bali Kumbat and Bali Nyonga continued for another century. It was not until April 1966 that a long-awaited reconciliation meeting was held in Bali Nyonga during which Galega II and Galabe III finally agreed to bury the hatchet and live together as brothers. It had taken three costly wars to get there. But even that was nothing compared to the upheaval that the white man was about to bring.

14   J.P Warnier, op. cit., pp. 545-546.

FIVE

The First Europeans
Bali and the Germans

The Berlin Conference of 1884, at which European diplomats boldly partitioned the African continent, is one of the most outrageous events in history. The cavalier spirit of that partition was revealed by the British Prime Minister, Lord Salisbury, in a supposedly humorous description of the work of the Anglo-French Commission on colonial boundaries in West Africa. Said he:

> we have been engaged in drawing lines on maps where no white man's foot ever trod; we have been giving away mountains and rivers and lakes to each other, only hindered by the small impediment that we never knew exactly where the mountains and rivers and lakes were.[1]

Or whether those features existed at all! Yet, notwithstanding that "small" impediment, the European countries coldly carved up the entire continent of Africa into colonies and private estates of all shapes and sizes. No part was left untouched, and many were appropriated years before the white man actually set foot on them. Such was the case of the Bamenda grassfields which became part of the German protectorate of Kamerun even before the first German arrived there.

---

1 Speech at a Mansion House dinner after formal signature of Anglo-French Convention of 1890. cf. J.C. Anene, *The International Boundaries of Nigeria*, (London; Longman, 1970), p. 3.

Life in these grassfields, as elsewhere on the African continent, has never been the same since.

Zintgraff in Bali

It is a manifestation of the spirit of adventure in the scramble for Africa that the first German to reach the Bamenda grassfields was not a government official, but a bearded explorer called Eugen Zintgraff. Yet his coming was of such immense significance that the story of his passage is now inseparable from the history of the Bamenda grassfields in the mid-nineteenth century. Not only was he the very first white man ever seen in the area, but he was also the harbinger of a new civilisation that would gradually take the people hostage.

Arrival and First Impressions

The first encounter with the white man was full of curiosity and suspicion. In early January 1889 when news came from Bamessong that there was a strange creature, perhaps a spirit about, Galega dispatched a group of "chĭntèd," including Doh Ndudina, Fòntɔ', and Tutuwàn Ngu, to see the sight. They were instructed to ascertain whether it was a man, and if so to bring him to Bali. So, the men rushed to Bamessong and after inspecting Zintgraff's physique and watching him eat some of their food, they were satisfied that he was probably a man, if of very poor complexion. They invited him to Bali, taking great care that he got to the presence of the Fon in one piece — and in broad daylight!

During the half-day march, Zintgraff pondered the nature of the Bali. His wanderings in Africa had not turned up anything like them yet. He was keenly impressed by their quiet self-possession and dignified hospitality. But he was a little anxious because "for the first time he had met Africans who looked at him straight in the eye."[2] If the Bali were surprised by his sight, they did not show it.

And so after a fleet-footed march from Bamessong, the first white man arrived in Bali Nyonga, to the witness of thousands. Zintgraff himself later described the spectacle of that arrival and his first encounter

2   E.M. Chilver, *Zintgraff's Explorations in Bamenda*, (Buea: Government Printer, 1966), p. 2.

with Galega I as follows:

> before us and gently rising, lay a large open square, lined on
> two sides with huts, into which numerous lanes led from
> different directions. In front of us was the extensive com-
> pound of the chief, hidden by finely woven mat walls and
> overhung by shady trees. On the upper side of the square
> squatted about 2000 warriors, their dane guns and spears
> upright between their knees, in perfect silence. Finally, the
> chief appeared, crossing the high threshold of the gate with
> slow, measured tread....[3]

Galega was a big and well-fleshed man, whose erect, powerful
and well-knit figure belied his sixty-odd years. He took a closer look
at the bearded German and decided at once that the white man was
an asset for the future. He was convinced about the publicity value of
a man whose sight aroused so much curiosity, and he imagined that
his rivals might even be scared by this latest acquisition. So Galega
not only invited Zintgraff to stay but tried to persuade him not to
visit other chiefdoms. Perhaps the most controversial period of Bali
history was about to begin, a period of collaboration with the white
man which started with solidarity on both sides and ended in confused
and conflicting interests on either side.

In their subsequent meetings, Zintgraff discovered that Galega was
not only a man of excellent manners but also a shrewd and observant
ruler, not the kind of man to be led easily by any European but a man
with whom one required the utmost tact and care. He was a very
ambitious man as well, with territorial aspirations far in excess of his
existing kingdom. According to Zintgraff, Galega I had the intention
of making himself the paramount ruler of the entire grassfields. To that
effect he sought to present himself as the chief arbitrator of disputes
between neighbouring tribes. And, in addition to his army of 5000, he
looked to European friendship and support to back up his influence

3   Eugen Zintgraff, *Nord Kamerun*, (Berlin, 1895), pp. 181-183.

and remove any doubt as to the enforceability of his arbitration.[4]

Zintgraff gladly welcomed Galega's friendship. The Bali connection was equally important to him. He was impressed by the discipline of the people, the fertility of the country and its nearness to perceived sources of ivory. Most importantly perhaps, he believed he had found in Galega a powerful ruler with rational impulses who could be a loyal, if interested, ally. The idea of establishing a German station in Bali Nyonga began to impress him. He did not want to miss the opportunity of using Galega's influence to foster the aims of the German Government, his employers since 1886.

The creation of the German station in Bali Nyonga impressed Galega as well, and he personally supervised the frantic efforts of his people to build it. In only six weeks, the station was complete — forty houses in all, including a mansion for Zintgraff himself.

Bali Nyonga as a German Station

Zintgraff imagined the hinterland of the German Kamerun as a vast reserve of natural and human resources. He thought there were immense quantities of ivory and palm products stored away in an area that could also constitute a big market for German exports. He perceived the opening up of the hinterland of the Protectorate, especially the Bamenda grassfields, primarily in economic terms, with the threefold objective to secure the diversion of trade from British Calabar to German Douala; establish a line of stations running into the unexplored interior which would draw native trade to the coast; and open up that interior for the recruitment of labour for the plantations of the south. Vital to this plan was a protected route to the interior, later referred to as the Mundame-Bali route.

The achievement of this threefold objective was the purpose of Zintgraff's second mission to the Bamenda grassfields. He had returned to Germany in early 1890 and had so forcefully argued his case at the German Colonial Office that the Government decided to send out a new expedition to Kamerun, together with a trading mission.

---

4   Ibid, pp. 203-341 passim.

Significantly, Zintgraff was given control of all political and military decisions affecting both expeditions. So, on 9 December 1890, Zintgraff arrived Bali on a more definite mission in the Bamenda grassfields to: cement the friendly relations with the chiefs; maintain peace and order in the hinterland; open secure caravan routes to the coast; and channel the trade of the hinterland along these routes to the Kamerun coast.[5]

The success of this grand design depended on Zintgraff's rapport with the people of the Kamerun hinterland. It was a rapport that the Germans found difficult to establish sometimes because their colour gave them away. So, they needed to rely on someone who not only knew the people, but could gain their confidence and exercise influence over them. They turned to Galega I. As the eminent ruler of a large kingdom, in an area that was divided into tiny tribes, Galega's friendship was invaluable to the Germans. Zintgraff understood to what extent Galega cherished his personal power and the strength of his kingdom. He was held in such godly esteem that Zintgraff reckoned the Bali Nyonga could become an indispensable ally if the Germans made use of his friendship and loyalty. And Zintgraff realized that the most effective way of achieving this was to increase Galega's power, even if only apparently! In fact, with time, the power of the Bali Nyonga was perceived as the major determinant of the German success in the Bamenda grassfields: the stronger they were, the easier it would be for German interests to penetrate the grassfields.

There seemed no stronger advocate of Bali power than Zintgraff himself, who, in a memorandum to the German government in 1889, urged "the establishment of a Commissionership in Bali, for the general administration of the grassfields."[6]

The explorer saw this as the best means of putting Galega's power and influence at the service of German interests. The aims of the proposed Commissionership were to protect European traders and missionaries; secure the caravan route; and unite the divided grassfields tribes under Galega I.[7] Zintgraff was recommending the erection of

5   Ibid., pp. 344-356.
6   Ibid., p. 341.
7   Ibid., p. 342.

Bali Nyonga into a full-fledged German station, in which capacity it would become the headquarters of the Bamenda grassfields, the source of political and military direction, the carrefour of trade and labour, and the hub of the German colonial enterprise in the grassfields. The German firm, Jantzen and Thormahlen, opened a factory there. They were followed by the Basler missionaries, who soon converted Bali into a church and education centre as well.

The success of those ventures depended on Galega's loyalty to his German connexions. In this regard the monarch seemed loyal to a fault. Zintgraff was held in very high esteem at the palace and throughout the kingdom where he was popularly referred to as "Fòmbolìŋgòŋ," one who mollifies the land. The story goes that once when a rumour circulated that another whiteman, suspected to be an Englishman, was warring in the forest area, Galega proposed to Zintgraff that if the stranger was not a German they should both attack him and divide his property.

Zintgraff was terrified, fearing that such conspiracies left no white man safe in the Bamenda grassfields. After all, in the partition that had brought them to Africa the British and the Germans were not enemies but partners, who treated their hosts with equal disdain.

Galega realised that his desire to please his guest had been grossly misconstrued. To make amends he offered Zintgraff the pact of blood brotherhood, usually contracted by intimate friends under serious circumstances. The ceremony itself was elaborately traditional: cuts were made on their arms and a paste of chewed kola and cubeb pepper was smeared on the incisions which both men licked; then blood from the cuts was poured into a pot of palm wine. Each drank from the wine and swore an oath of mutual protection. To break this oath meant that the transgressor's belly would swell and in nine days he would die horribly.[8] Galega used the occasion to proclaim the philosophy of his relationship with the German:

> you came like a little cock into my house, white man, and I

8   Pat Ritzenthaler, op. cit., p. 33.

could have easily killed you and taken your valuables... But I will not harm you. It is better to obtain the knowledge of the whites and to have them as friends to our lasting benefit, than to take short-lived advantage of them by robbery.[9]

The Zintgraff - Galega Treaty, 1891

But the blood pact was only a temporary lull in Zintgraff's anxiety about Galega. He had become increasingly uneasy, upon realising that the Fon had discovered the real motives of the Germans. But he soon found what he perceived to be an effective insurance against any changes in Galega's intentions. He exhorted the German government that "provided we support and intelligently favour Galega's plans, which are at least in full agreement with ours, it would not be too difficult to bind him lastingly to our interests."[10]

To this effect, Zintgraff presented to Galega a draft treaty for approval and signature. It was a typical colonial treaty, a document of grandiose intent and double-meaning substance. The aim of the treaty was, ostensibly, "to bring the Bali tribe to such power and influence as will enable it to lead the tribes in northern Kamerun."[11] But in reality, the treaty sanctioned the gross abdication of Galega's powers over his kingdom. The Fon was to surrender to Zintgraff all his powers of life and death, of peace and war within the Bali realm. And he would implement all decisions in those matters taken by Zintgraff.[12] Only then would "the establishment, recognition and protection of Galega's position as the paramount chief of the surrounding tribes of the northern Kamerun hinterland" be assured.[13] And as payment for loyal compliance with the terms of the treaty, Galega was granted an official salary from the proceeds of regular tax raised from neighbouring villages and from duty payable by Germans passing through Bali.[14]

The Zintgraff-Galega treaty of August 1891 was not a negotiated

---

9   Eugen Zintgraff, op. cit., p. 202.
10   Ibid., p. 342.
11   Zintgraff-Galega Treaty, 1891, Preamble.
12   Articles I and II.
13   Art. II.
14   Art. IV.

agreement with input from both sides. It was written by the German singlehandedly, outlining and clearly overstating his prerogatives, and converting the powerful Fon into an employee of the colonial government, a sort of tădmànjì in his own kingdom. Zintgraff succeeded in minimising Galega's power by pretending to build it up. No wonder, Galega's part of the bargain was decisively vague: his sphere of influence would now extend to the tribes of the northern Kamerun hinterland, a geographical expression without limit or description. What was more, Galega was being nominally placed at the head of this nondescript body when, by the same treaty, he was being stripped of his essential powers over his proper kingdom!

It is difficult to understand how a man as alert as Galega, who had fought many wars to build his kingdom could give it all to a stranger in exchange for an intangible friendship and petty cash. In the tortuous translation of the treaty, it is probable that the finer details were lost to Galega I. It is also possible that Zintgraff might have given the Fon many verbal assurances.

The Zintgraff-Galega treaty was a typical colonial mirage where a bearded European, without title or mandate, arrogated for himself the powers of life and death in an African kingdom that he barely knew. It was dishonest enough to ask someone to "sign" a document in a language that he did not understand and therefore could not ascertain its terms. To be bound by such a document was a massive fraud. Indications are that when Galega I put three crosses at the foot of the page to indicate his consent, it was not clear to him that he was signing away his administrative, political and military powers over his kingdom, and putting paid to all future territorial ambitions.

Unfortunately, it has not been possible to reconstruct Galega's exact understanding of the treaty, since the only records of the proceedings are those left by Zintgraff. Besides, the treaty was highly personalised, referring to the contracting parties by name instead of by office, in the manner of a private agreement between them. Still, it was approved by the German government as the basis of their policy in the Bamenda grassfields.

Bali Nyonga in German Policy

There were two contrasting facets of German policy towards Bali Nyonga. On the one hand they sought to consolidate Bali influence so as to win Galega's confidence and use his prestige to penetrate the Bamenda grassfields. In that case, Bali Nyonga was projected to serve as middlemen between the Germans and the rest of the grassfields. As the German Governor pointed out:

> without doubt an influential position for the chiefs orientated towards the government is easy and advantageous for the transmission of the station's orders and instructions to the large bulk of the population... Consequently, the purposeful strengthening of Galega's prestige rightly formed one of the main tasks of the administration.[15]

But on the other hand, the Germans sought to dispose of Bali influence once they could find their way in the grassfields, and when it appeared to them that the Bali were becoming too powerful and too independent. German policy towards Bali Nyonga was thus finely balanced between encouraging and inhibiting Galega's influence.

Conquest and Expansion

From the very onset, Bali Nyonga seemed completely indispensable to the Germans. Their expeditions into the grassfields, coming as they did from the south, were bound to cross Galega's kingdom, which controlled the gateway into those grassfields. To reach the hinterland, the Germans had to fight their way forward or make peace with Galega. They chose to make peace, knowing that the best interests of warriors are sometimes served by peace. And especially as Galega offered peace, not war.

The Germans welcomed Galega's peace and used it to prepare the anticipated wars of conquest. Their alliance with the Bali gave them the confidence and even increased their willingness to fight such wars.

15   Comments of the Governor on the 1911 *Bamenda Divisional Annual Report*, Buea, 10 July 1912.

Moreso after Galega solemnly assured Zintgraff following their blood pact that "Your friends are my friends, your foes my foes."[16] And Galega I was not a man of half measures.

One of the main attractions that the Germans found in Bali, apart from their hospitality, was their military prowess. Germans know a good soldier when they see one. Zintgraff had been more than impressed by the size and discipline of the Bali army, and the dexterity with which they performed their complex drills. But there was something else in the Bali that Zintgraff had not seen before in Kamerun: they had so much natural military talent! So much that with a little formal training in basic German war tactics, Zintgraff reckoned they could become a formidable force indeed.

The training of the Bali army was directed by Lieutenant Franz Hutter, a Bavarian artillery officer who joined Zintgraff in 1891. A select crack force of 200 Bali soldiers received daily training in disciplined firing in a rifle-range that had been built close to the German station. Meanwhile at the town green, another German soldier carefully drilled the 100-strong, musket-armed bodyguard of the Fon.

The progress of the trainees delighted Hutter, who confessed that the results far exceeded his expectations.[17] Little wonder that Zintgraff credited the Bali troops with being "as quick off the mark as our German recruits."[18]

Curiously, the drills involved in training were not limited to the army. Military discipline soon became a way of life throughout the chiefdom. And it was not only a matter for the adults. The Germans also taught Bali children a thing or two about the military, as Max Moisel later reported:

> In the afternoon, as I was wandering around with my camera, the missionaries asked me to photograph their school classes. The children were rapidly called out of school and arranged.

16   Eugen Zintgraff, op. cit., p. 360.
17   Franz Hutter, *Wanderungen und Forschungen im Nord-Hinterland von Kamerun*, Braunschweig, 1902, pp. 17-27.
18   Eugen Zintgraff, op. cit., p. 218.

As the light required a change of place, Missionary Ernst, to my surprise, did this to staccato Prussian Commands: on the order Stillstand! (Atten-tion!) 200 or so heels clicked together, and all hands were at once placed along where, in a German boy, his trouser seam would have been. Likewise with other commands — Linksum! (Left, about-turn!), Battalion march! To the right, march; Battalion, halt! Eyes front! This drill made an odd impression on me since, apart from these words of command, the Bali lads did not understand a word of German.[19]

All that training was just as well because Zintgraff and his Bali allies had some rather difficult wars to fight in the early days of the German penetration of the Bamenda grassfields.

Contrary to the warm Bali welcome, German presence was fiercely resisted by many grassfields tribes, notably the city-states of Mankon and Bafut. The ferocity of their resistance was a function of their animosity towards Bali Nyonga, with whom they competed for domination of the grassfields. Zintgraff's vaunted friendship with the dreaded Galega ensured that they could not look at him with any sympathy at all. And the Bali did their best to create as much misunderstanding as possible between Zintgraff and their rivals. Inevitably wars were fought, as much the result of these misunderstandings as of their genuine desires not to give ground to the Whiteman whom they saw as wearing a Bali mask.

The Mankon War

The Mankon War of January 1891, the first German military engagement in the Bamenda grassfields, was a pre-emptive campaign, intended to clear the way for a massive strike against Bafut. Apart from a few unsubstantiated insinuations, the events that led to the war had no direct bearing on Mankon itself. At best, the attack could be seen as a deterrent strike.

---

19   Max Moisel, *Deutsche Kolonialzeitung*, op. cit.

Upon his return to Bali in December 1890, Zintgraff decided to open up the interior of the Bamenda grassfields where large supplies of ivory were believed to exist. On Christmas day, he dispatched two Vai envoys, accompanied by two Bali guides, to Bafut to announce the coming of an expedition from the Jantzen and Thormahlen company, who had already established a firm in Bali, to open trade links with Bafut. But the two Vai boys were mysteriously killed. At first a Bali conspiracy was suspected whereby the Vai messengers would have been murdered by their Bali companions so as to incriminate the Bafut and sabotage their dealings with Zintgraff. But when it was proved that the men had actually been murdered by the Bafut, new explanations began to emerge. The Bali suggested that the killings had been instigated by the Mankon chief to sabotage any entente between Bali and Bafut and discourage Zintgraff's men from trading with the latter. The Mankon chief is said to have warned the Bafut Chief of the dangers of the German presence and that Zintgraff was preparing a huge invasion of Bafut, as part of which the Vai messengers had been sent to spy on them and plant dangerous medicines in the land. Thereupon the Bafut angrily killed them.[20]

Mankon and Bafut traditions differ with this account. They argue that the deaths were the result of insulting demands made by the messengers. The story goes that when the Fon of Bafut asked the envoys what the Germans wanted, they responded that as punishment for refusing to show Zintgraff the way north on his previous visit, the Bafut would now have to pay a fine of five elephant tusks, five leopard skins and five women. Abumbi I was enraged. Then one of the Vai boys added insult to injury by holding out a clip of cartridges as a threat of war if the demands were not met. But Abumbi refused to be blackmailed. The two Vai messengers were killed, their heads stuck to the gateposts of the palace, and their Bali companions sent home to deliver the message to their black and white masters.[21]

News of the killings caused a stir in Bali, turning into fury when Zintgraff's demands for ten ivories and five oxen as compensation for

20   Eugene Zintgraff, op. cit., pp. 358-364.
21   Pat Ritzenthaler, op. cit., p. 40.

the murders was defiantly rejected with the provocative challenge: "If you are men, come and fetch them yourselves."[22] That was interpreted as throwing down the gauntlet, and as Zintgraff insisted on avenging his Vai messengers it became clear that war was imminent.

However, in an unexpected turn of events, Zintgraff decided to attack Mankon first. This sudden change of heart is difficult to explain. It has been suggested that he decided to punish Fomukong's men for the alleged machinations that led to the murder of the Vai messengers. But it seems that he was under the impression that effective action could not be taken against Bafut unless Mankon, its close ally, was immobilised. And he convinced Galega to the idea.

At an elaborate War Council in Galega's palace, the attack on Mankon was scheduled for 31 January 1891. So, on the 30th a huge force of nearly 3000 men set out from Bali, accompanied by Zintgraff and four other Germans. The campaign followed a typical Bali battle plan, although it took place under the banner of the German flag and not the Bali "tutuwàn". The army assembled at Bangwa [Nsongwa], which served as "Ntânbèd" for the occasion, and broke up into three sectors — the two traditional "Manjòŋs" under Tita Nji and Tita Gwenjang, and a new sector comprising the Widikum, Vai and Europeans. Tita Gwenjang was assigned the duty of circling Mankon to cut off prospective reinforcements from Bafut, while the other two sectors advanced on the target frontally.

When all three sectors linked up again at the marketplace, the fate of Mankon was sealed. They stormed the town, crushing every form of resistance. By the afternoon when they withdrew, Mankon was in flames, with over 600 casualties.

But the war was not over. Although the town was burnt, the Mankon people did not give up. The first strike had failed to knock them out completely. And they gained new heart from massive reinforcements that finally came through from Bafut after Tita Gwenjang's force had withdrawn. The combined Mankon-Bafut force stalked the enemy and caught up with the bulk of the Bali army at Bangwa,

22   Eugen Zintgraff, op. cit., p. 364

prematurely celebrating their victory. They engaged them in a fierce counterattack, in which the fresher Bafut troops played a decisive role. The attack was all the more devastating because the Bali were caught with their arms unloaded. The German officer in-charge of supplies, Lt. von Sprangenberg, had suspended the distribution of further ammunition, thinking that the battle was over. So, when the counterattack began, over 100 Bali soldiers were killed before their side could return fire. The plight of the Bali was worsened by a rebellion of the Widikum villages of Bangwa, Mbatu and Baforchu, whose soldiers suddenly changed camps and joined the Bafut and Mankon instead. The Mankon counterattack nearly became the main story of the war. But the Bali were let off the hook as the falling darkness made it impossible to distinguish friend from foe. Still, they lost nearly 200 men, including all the Germans, with the exception of Zintgraff who had earlier returned to Bali by a different route.

The Mankon war was a disaster for all involved: Mankon was reduced to rubble, but the Germans who ordered the campaign paid dearly for it, and the Bali who executed it had little cause to celebrate, not even after Tita Gwenjang returned with an elite force the following day and laid waste the treacherous villages.

The Bafut War, 1901

The Mankon war was a costly diversion from Zintgraff's aim of subduing Bafut. So costly that the Bafut expedition was put off for another ten years. By then, neither Zintgraff nor Galega I were there to see it happen. The former had died in December 1897 on his way home on sick leave. The latter outlived him by a few years but died in early 1901. He was succeded by Fonyonga II, who was no stranger to the conflict — as Tita Gwenjang, he had been the most outstanding general in the Mankon war. And he inherited his father's friendship with the Germans. Still, war against Bafut put him in an awkward situation: he had a long personal relationship with Abumbi I, with whom he often exchanged gifts. Fighting him was like fighting a friend. But Fonyonga also knew that their two peoples had been bitter rivals, who were bound to cross paths sooner or later.

As for the Germans, the loss of Zintgraff had not made them

any less keen to subdue Bafut, especially as opening up the Kamerun hinterland remained a major plank of their colonial policy.

In November 1901, a large expedition commanded by Pavel arrived Bali, partly to consolidate German hold on the hinterland and partly to settle old scores from the war of 1891, with Mankon and Bafut. The expedition was joined by thousands of Bali soldiers as it set out on its Bafut campaign. It marched first to Mankon where it overran and burnt the town for the second time when the indemnity of ivory demanded was not forthcoming. Then they continued swiftly unto Bafut.

Their arrival was no surprise. Abumbi had been warned of the invasion by a Mankon messenger, and had mobilised his troops accordingly, after sending off the women and children to hide in the hills.

The ensuing battle raged for weeks. In spite of their inferior armaments, the Bafut offered heroic resistance under the command of Abumbi himself. They constantly shifted from one valley to another, making it difficult for the Germans to use their superior fire power to good effect. In fact, at one point they were so demoralised by the elusive guerrilla tactics of the Bafut that they sued for peace, an offer that Abumbi rejected, wildly over-estimating his strength. That turned out to be a very costly mistake because the Germans, now resigned to a protracted war, dug their heels in and fought on. And the more they knew the terrain, the more effective they became. In the end, Bafut ran out of cover and ammunition; they fled to the hills as one by one their villages went up in flames. They wandered in the bush for about six months, roaming as far north as the Menchum Falls, before Abumbi decided, in a flash of martyrdom, to save his people from starvation by turning himself in. He showed up at the new station at Bamenda where he was promptly arrested and banished to Douala for one year,[23] thereby ending years of Bafut resistance to the German penetration. It had been a very costly resistance indeed. The Bafut war had claimed nearly 1500 casualties from Bafut and Mankon, with 600

23   Pat Ritzenthaler, op. cit., pp. 69-73.

taken prisoner and another 500 levied as forced labourers.

In the Bafut war, as in the Mankon campaign ten years earlier, the Bali contribution was significant. After avoiding it for years, Bali Nyonga finally took on its leading rivals, not on its own account but on account of its friendship with the Germans, as Bali became the centre of the German scheme for the Bamenda grassfields. The Bafut war was the last major obstacle to the German penetration of the grassfields. Having established themselves, they now had to figure out how to administer the "pacified" regions. And in this as well, Bali Nyonga would be the centrepiece of their strategy.

Administration

One of the main purposes of opening up the Kamerun hinterland was to create and maintain a steady supply of labour to the German plantations in the south and a steady source of income to the colonial government in the form of taxes. The problems of penetration had convinced the Germans that they could not do this all by themselves. So initially they co-opted some indigenous rulers into a new "ruling class" to act on their behalf in the recruitment of labour and the collection of taxes, with the German station serving to coordinate these efforts and convey the proceeds to the headquarters.

The Fon of Bali was the most prominent member of this pro-German group of grassfields rulers. Although he had no defined administrative functions within the colonial set-up he was nonetheless expected and encouraged to administer his domains in a way as to facilitate the goals of the colonial government. In this regard, German policy underwent some sensible modifications. Unlike Zintgraff who, in the treaty of 1891, had cunningly tried to rob Galega of his royal powers, later Germans, with more knowledge of the land and more versed in colonial administration, treated Fonyonga with more respect. They acknowledged his paramountcy, even if they sought to use it to their own ends. On 13 January 1903, "in consideration of his faithful services," Fonyonga II was given a letter of protection by the German Governor, Puttkamer, according to which the Fon of Bali was placed under the "full protection of the Imperial Government," and all Europeans residing at Bali or travelling through it were required "to afford Chief Fonyonga of Bali every possible assistance."[24] And on 15 June 1905, before an assembly of 47 grassfields chiefs, the new station commander, Captain Hans Glauning, formally proclaimed Fonyonga II as the paramount ruler of the 31 villages of his realm.[25] The villages included:

1. Babadju	12. Batibo	23. Baforchu
2. Bamessinge	13. Bamyensi	24. Baba
3. Bangang	14. Bamunung	25. Bangwa
4. Pinyin	15. Bamenjong	26. Bafomessang
5. Bamessong	16. Batabi	27. Mbatu
6. Bamowa	17. Banja	28. Fongwen
7. Bamunyi	18. Bossa	29. Banti
8. Bessi	19. Fonyam	30. Fongu (Babadju)
9. Guzang	20. Forbang	31. Bambunji
10. Bambo	21. Take	
11. Bamefa	22. Fongu	

Relations between Bali and the Germans had never been better. The Germans knew that by recognising and protecting Fonyonga's position, they would secure his loyalty and increase his effectiveness as an agent in recruiting labour and collecting taxes. Any attempt to undermine his authority was harshly dealt with; the chief of Batibo was exiled to Banyo in September 1910 for insubordination to Fonyonga.

In 1907, the German Government introduced a hut tax in the grassfields, to complement and gradually to replace the supply of labour. It was an extension of a poll tax that had been in operation in the Douala District since 1903, and it was introduced to undercut mounting disaffection caused by massive recruitment of labour for the coast. Fonyonga usually received tax tickets for all the villages of his realm, which he then distributed to them through his tǎdmànjì, and a 10% stipend upon collection and payment of the taxes to the station.

24 E.M. Chilver, "Paramountcy and Protection in the Cameroons," op. cit., pp. 494-495.
25 Ibid., pp. 496-499.

The Fon took his tax responsibilities seriously. He frequently summoned subject chiefs to bring in their tax returns, and if these were not forthcoming, he would pay the tax from his pocket pending later reimbursement so as to protect his subjects and please the Germans. Unfortunately, the reimbursement of pre-paid taxes was often a source of bitter argument with the subject chiefs. These difficulties were later taken as justification for a new German policy that would have serious consequences for Bali Nyonga itself.

The new policy began in early 1906 when the German administration began the forceful removal and resettlement of some Meta villages inside Bali. The sheer brutality of the operation surprised many: the villages were simply razed to the ground, sometimes without warning, and their inhabitants herded into Bali for resettlement. In all, eleven Widikum villages were uprooted from their original homes and bundled into Bali.[26] These included:

1. Fongwe (including Fombu and Mungen)
2. Bossa
3. Forbang
4. Fonyam
5. Fongu
6. Take
7. Banja (including Bakam)
8. Bambunji
9. Bamyensi
10. Bamenjong
11. Batabi

The rationale of the programme, which according to Moisel increased the population of Bali to over 20,000 by 1907,[27] was not known. It has been suggested that the aim of the scheme was to facilitate the collection of taxes from Bali. However, there is nothing to show that tax collection from the resettled villages had been deficient before 1906 or that it improved sensibly thereafter. It has also been suggested that the purpose of resettlement was to enhance Fonyonga's authority over his vassals. Yet the villages involved had no outstanding history of insubordination. In fact, the forceful resettlement of eleven

26 W.E. Hunt, Confidential Report N° C2/21, Bamenda, 10/6/21.
27 Max Moisel, "Ein Expedition in die Grashochlander Mittel-Kamerun," in *Deutsche Kolonialzeitung*, Sonderbeilage Zu N° 15 vom 11 April 1908.

Meta villages within Bali has remained one of the enigmatic policies of the German era. It stirred deep resentment, leading to the bitterness that subsequently characterised relations between Bali Nyonga and its neighbours.

Labour Supply

The most significant role of Bali Nyonga within the German colonial scheme was as a source of cheap plantation labour. The centrepiece of the colonial enterprise in Kamerun was plantation development in the coastal areas, operated by a few companies, notably the "Westafrikanische Pflanzungs-Gesellschaft Victoria" [WAPV] and the "Gesellschaft Nordwest-Kamerun" [GNK]. For both companies, the constant supply of cheap labour was vital for success.

Previously, the Germans relied on foreign labour from Ghana and Liberia. But labour from such distant sources was difficult to recruit and expensive to maintain. So Zintgraff argued for their replacement with local labour, especially the sturdy natives of the Kamerun hinterland. This was one of the areas where Galega would be most useful to the Germans, and on his third visit to Bali in June 1896 Zintgraff lost no time in negotiating terms with Galega for the large-scale supply of labour to the coast. The details of the contract were worked out by Zintgraff's companion, Max Esser, who noted in his memoirs that when the labour question was broached, "Galega did not want to hear it, saying he needed his people for defence."[28] But promises of personal wealth and assurances that he could also recruit from vassal villages won him over. The agreement provided that Galega would send several hundred men to the coast each year, for whom the government would pay him a head tax for every man, at departure and on return.[29]

The first beneficiary of this arrangement was the WAPV, which received the initial batch of Bali recruits in June 1897. The company even acquired a plot in Bali on which it hoped to build a factory as a base for its operations. The agreement with Galega provided for a European recruiting mission to visit this base every two years.

28   Max Esser, *An der Westkuste Afrikas*, Leipzig, 1898, p. 135.
29   Ibid., p. 146.

And so Galega became the leading grassfields agent for supplying plantation labour to the Germans. He used his kingdom liberally for this purpose, only restrained by what work force he needed for his own public works. Initially the WAPV was his only client. But this exclusiveness was challenged in 1900 with the establishment of the GNK which sent its own agent to Bali to discuss with Galega the prospects of setting up a factory as a permanent basis for monopolistic recruitment of labour. The WAPV responded by reiterating its own monopoly claims over Bali and immediately dispatching a resident agent there to secure those interests.

But the German companies soon realised that their quarrels could only distract from their goals. They sorted out their differences by simply increasing the quota of labour to be supplied by Galega. In order to satisfy the exorbitant demands, Galega and Fonyonga after him resorted to mass recruitments, with Bali soldiers launching indiscriminate labour raids throughout the kingdom. The figures are harrowing: in 1904 alone Fonyonga II supplied as many as 1700 able-bodied men to the plantations, and a census of 1912 revealed that there were no more than 4000 men left in Bali. Reviewing this cruel drain of the Bali population the station commander, Adametz, candidly observed that "the flower of the Bali nation lies on the Cameroon Mountain."[30]

Yet the Germans were not concerned with how the natives were used, so long as they achieved their aims. In his obsession with the security of the route to the interior, Zintgraff even proposed to create Bali settlements in Mundame, Batome and Banyang. He estimated that the Mundame-Bali road would be completely secured because "a homogeneous element under the orders of a powerful inland chief will reside there."[31] It says much of the intentions of the Germans that such a move could have been contemplated at all. The Germans were seeking to satisfy present needs, even if that would cause severe future disaffection.

The excessive corvee, for which Fonyonga was encouraged to

---

30   *Report by Bamenda Stationschef,* Adametz, 13 May 1913.
31   *Letter to Chancellor von Caprivi,* 4/3/1982, c.f. E.M. Chilver, Diary on Bali Nyonga, 1960, Ms. pp 2-3.

behave like a tyrant, was bound to sap morale and alienate even his own people. For the time being, however, the Germans seemed well pleased that Bali was living up to its expectations as a resourceful labour market for the German plantations.

Missionary Activity

Evangelisation, the familiar train of colonial enterprise, which usually brought a moral face to a largely material undertaking, arrived Bali Nyonga in May 1903 after Fonyonga's kingdom had already been established as a German station and a booming labour market. Significantly, Bali had been recommended to the Basler Mission as a prospective missionary post by a German plantation owner, Dr Esser, who had been lavishly entertained by Galega I in the 1890s. He saw the grassfields kingdom as a potential source of labour for his plantations and urged the church to establish a mission there as a means for securing the work force for future recruitment.[32] To which might be added the desire to push Christianity further up country and halt the downward spread of Islam.

Owing to shortage of funds, however, the mission did not open in Bali immediately. It was not until November 1902 that three Basler missionaries, Schuler, Keller and Spellenberg visited Bali and confirmed it as a suitable site for the grassfields mission. Following that visit the first resident missionaries, Ernst, Leimbacher and Keller, arrived Bali in May 1903. They all lived in Fonyonga's palace until a suitable house was built for them.

The missionaries lost no time in beginning their work. A temporary church was built within one month of their arrival, and the evangelisation of Bali Nyonga began in earnest. Regular Sunday service started on 6 August 1905, and on 20 November 1908 the first 32 converts were baptised. These were followed by another 39 in 1909, including four women, and by 1914 Leimbacher had completed the magnificent red-brick church that is still in use in Bali today.

Gradually, the mission became another of the centripetal

---

32   Harry Rudin, *Germans in the Cameroons, 1884-1914* (London: Jonathan Cape, 1938), pp. 365-366.

forces of Bali. The missionary Ferdinand Ernst, popularly known as "Fònyŭŋchù" because of his luxuriant beard, established very good relations with the Fon, serving as his adviser and the new voice of Bali at the Station. In return, he received lavish royal patronage of his mission: Fonyonga gave them large expanses of land, and even declared Sunday as a day of rest for all his subjects.

This patronage notwithstanding, there remained some doubt as to the depth of Fonyonga's belief in the new faith, knowing the extent to which he had been influenced by the philosophical Galega I. As he once remarked to Zintgraff: "Given the uncertainty and fickleness of human affairs, let one eat and drink enough on every one of God's days, so that whatever happens in the course of the day, nothing can spoil the appetite."[33] He was even more pragmatic in his perception of Christianity. When Zintgraff tried to sell the new religion to the old monarch, Galega's response was spiced with practical wisdom:

> Man only knows what he sees. Knowledge is the only right basis of belief and everything else is but useless speculation; but if the missionaries came to my land I could, if I could see its advantages, be willingly baptised, but would not exclude other beliefs... but I wish to be a friend of the whiteman and take the good from where it is to be found.[34]

The missionaries did not reach Bali in Galega's time, but there was a great deal of speculation as to how much of his materialist philosophy had been imbibed by his successor. The fact that Fonyonga himself never thought of getting baptised says something of the influence that Galega had on him.

Fonyonga was more interested in the side benefits of the church, just as Galega might have been. When the missionaries opened a boy's school in Bali in 1907, he not only attended the inauguration but sent three of his sons into the first batch of 63 pupils. He was so fascinated by the school that at the age of forty-five he learnt how to

---

33   Cf. Max Moisel, op. cit.
34   Ibid.

read and write. He personally rounded up boys for the school and pursued runaways.[35] He gave the brightest pupils pocket money and encouraged them to be recruited as teachers in the vernacular schools that sprang up in neighbouring villages. In the morning, such boys would be taught by the Germans, and in the afternoon, they would go out to teach in the vernacular schools.

Yet, in spite of all his enthusiasm, Fonyonga did not succeed in changing the initial attitude of his people towards the school. In view of the amount of corporal punishment meted out there, the Bali saw the school as a corvee best suited for the sons of "niwɔmbè." When it became clear to them that education was the bet of the future, they needed quick steps to make amends.

Nevertheless, the presence of the Basler mission added a new dimension to the importance of Bali Nyonga. Fonyonga's kingdom became the spiritual and educational centre of the grassfields, the land of expedition to which children of the future were sent to be brought up. And it was from there that the other stations of the grassfields were opened, notably, Fumban, Bangwa, Bagam, We, Babungo, Bamenda, Bafut and Mbengwi.

Furthermore, the implantation of many missionary institutions during and after the German period was first tested in Bali. In 1936, a Catechist Training Centre was opened in Bali by the Reverend Adolf Vielhauer. It was transferred to Bafut in 1940 and to Nyasoso in 1952, where it later developed into a full-fledged Theological College. Similarly, a girl's school started in Bali by Miss Hummel was later transferred to Mbengwi and then to Bafut in 1937. The same school finally moved to Bamenda where Miss Lina Weber converted it into a Women Teachers Training Centre.

Perhaps the most important aspect of the new Bali power was the spread, through church and school, of its language, Mungaka. In spite of strong resistance from rival tribes and from the colonial government fearful of unduly extending Fonyonga's influence, the Basler Mission adopted Mungaka as the educational and evangelical language, thereby

35   Ibid.

spreading the Bali Nyonga language far beyond the kingdom. The Reverend Adolf Vielhauer published a collection of Bible stories in Mungaka in 1915, as a prelude to the herculean task of translating the Bible into Mungaka. In this latter job he was ably assisted by a team of Bali language experts, led by the Reverend Elisa Ndifon Gwansalla. The Mungaka version of the New Testament came out in 1933 and was revised in 1958, while the complete Bible in Mungaka was published in 1961, two years after the death of Vielhauer himself.

The Decline of Bali Influence

Association with the Germans is one of the most controversial aspects of Bali history. There have been contrasting views of this special relationship. Every Bali achievement during the German era was generously attributed to it — and every Bali failure, depending on which hill one stands to view the matter. It has been suggested that the Germans brought Bali to the height of its influence. Some even say that the Bali realm was entirely a German creation, raised from nothing and sustained at great cost. But the fact is that the Germans found a vast Bali realm, under the firm grip of the formidable Galega I. They brought that realm to the limelight, giving it far more publicity than it had — or needed.

The publicity was not gratuitous. And it would have been naive to expect that the German friendship could be without compensation of some kind. The Bali probably understood that the Germans had designs of their own. They could not have travelled so far for nothing. But the Bali also figured that their interests were better served by association with the Germans rather than in conflict with them. In a sense, they were competitors for the same resources, and when the colonial government prohibited trade monopolies and personal rights over ivory and other natural resources, Galega's economic situation was seriously undermined. He became dependent on money derived from court fines and tax commissions.

Impact of the German Association

As the excitement about the Germans subsided, it gradually became clear that every single aspect of their policy had a reverse side that was hardly as appealing as the one presented to the indigenes. And with time, the uglier faces of German policy began to be seen more frequently in and around Bali.

The ruthlessness of the German conquest, in which the Bali were often zealous accomplices, did much harm to their image. Having spotted the military instincts of Galega's men, the Germans eagerly used them to foster their own ends in wars that were very unpopular throughout the grassfields, and in which Bali participation was seen as a sell-out. Moreover, the campaigns were not always useful to Bali itself. The Mankon and Bafut wars were not programmed. Casualties were heavy, not evenly distributed throughout the kingdom. Support troops from vassal villages, whose experience of warfare was limited, suffered most in the reverse at Bangwa in 1891, prompting complaints that the Bali had sacrificed countless vassals in an unnecessary war. Meanwhile, the Bafut war ruined the budding friendship between Fonyonga II and Abumbi and renewed the hostility between their two chiefdoms. The German wars of "pacification" thus returned Bali to a war footing at a time when it needed to consolidate itself by seeking peace with its neighbours.

And the victories over their arch-rivals of Bafut and Mankon in those wars, which Bali would have thoroughly enjoyed at other times, seemed of little comfort now. They were German wars, resulting in barren victories for Bali.

But nothing epitomised the association of Bali and the Germans better than the presence of the German station in Bali. Fonyonga's involvement in the administration of the Bamenda grassfields on behalf of the Germans created unnecessary frictions with his own vassal chiefs. The system of "tǎdmànjì" which assured his suzerainty over them was no longer deemed to be sufficient. Fonyonga found himself interfering more and more in their internal affairs to explain the policy of the colonial government and transmit its instructions. However, the more he ran such errands, the more his aura diminished. His image was tarnished when it came to rounding up labour for the plantations. Most of them were taken by force, to destinations unknown to them. It was probably the most unpopular chore that the Fon of Bali ever had to perform, as he tore into families, separating husbands from their wives and children from their fathers, in order to satisfy the white man.

And even when the brutality of forced labour was replaced by a hut tax in 1907, Fonyonga's role as the chief tax collector did not endear him to the people. Squabbles over amounts of tax owed to him by his subject chiefs lost the Fon much respect and gradually those chiefs began not only to question his authority but also to resist his suzerainty. Several vassals saw the tax as replacement for the tribute that they normally paid to the Fon of Bali. They became increasingly reluctant to pay him any more tribute. His hold on the realm fatally began to slip. But at the same time, the Germans interpreted his difficulties in collecting the tax as resulting from inefficiency on his part.

The presence of the mission in Bali brought its own problems as well. The colonial government was increasingly irritated by the friendship between Fonyonga and the missionaries, especially by the constant interventions of Ernst on the Fon's behalf. And the adoption of Mungaka as the church and school language particularly worried colonial officials who feared that it would unduly extend the influence of Bali. At a conference with grassfields missionaries in 1912, the government obtained the replacement of Mungaka with Bamun as the evangelical medium for the grassfields.[36]

Initially, the Bali subjects took most of the changes introduced by the Germans with only mild protest, although one could see their anguish grow. It boiled over in 1906 when the Germans began the forced resettlement of some within Bali proper. And here again the target of their venom was Bali Nyonga and not the Germans. The subject villages suspected the resettlement plan as a Bali conspiracy to bring them right under Fonyonga's nose. Their bitterness with the policy, arising from the indignity of forced resettlement, radically transformed their relations with Bali. Several Widikum villages which

36   Harry Rudin op. cit., p. 358.

had accommodated Bali suzerainty in the past now resented the idea of losing their independence and living in Fonyonga's backyard. The resettlement policy sowed the seeds of the acrimonious land disputes that later plagued the history of Bali: for although most of the resettled villages eventually returned to their original sites, many stayed on to lay claim to the land on which they had been forcibly resettled in Bali.

Loss of Influence

The Germans were among the first to notice the early signs of unrest within Bali. They modified their attitudes accordingly. 1908 has been regarded as the year of dramatic change in German policy towards Bali. That change began with the loss of Fonyonga's staunchest ally in the colonial administration, Captain Glauning, the Bamenda station commander who died on 5 March. Anxious to make his own mark, his successor, Captain Menzel, decided to break with the practices of the past. He began by questioning the wisdom of the station's policy of relying so heavily on Fonyonga for the supply of labour and the collection of taxes. In his first report to the Governor, he recommended that with the death of Captain Glauning, "the only person with an accurate knowledge of the district, the station has to make a new start in establishing contact with the chiefs and in removing intermediaries [such as Fonyonga]."[37]

German suspicions of Bali were not new. As early as 1899 they had begun to seek counterweights to Galega's power. They disliked his independence and were worried by the entry of his people into the long-distance trade, the purpose for which the Germans were working so hard to "pacify" the interior. As it were, this was one of the kickbacks of the German connection. The Bali shrewdly exploited their role as middlemen between the Germans and the hinterland peoples, using German arms to defend their own trading parties to the coast. Those parties, often well-organised on departure cleverly broke up into individual traders when they reached the German factory at Mundame, selling small individual quantities of ivory to the

---

37   Cf. E.M. Chilver, *Paramountcy and Protection in the Cameroons*, p. 500.

same Germans for whom they made the acquisition of larger stocks virtually impossible. The Germans suspected something, and began to look for new allies. They transferred the station to Bamenda, hoping to demote Bali Nyonga from the centre to the periphery of grassfields politics. And in 1902, further grassfields stations were opened in Fumban and Banyo.

But it was not until 1908, with the death of both Glauning and Ernst, that a new policy was unleashed against Bali. Captain Menzel, the new station commander, concluded in his first report that the Bali realm could only be maintained by force; an exercise which would lead to a wasteful employment of the station's military resources. In other words, the Bali Nyonga sphere of influence was becoming cumbersome, a theme to which succeeding German officials would return time and time again. The Bali Nyonga decline had been launched.

The station's report of 7 May 1909 referred for the first time to the disaffection of the southern vassal villages of Bali — Bamessinge, Babadju, Bangang and Bamumbu — attributing it to the oppressive practices of Fonyonga II and recommending their separation from Bali. That recommendation was reiterated by the next station commander, von Raven, in his report of 4 August 1909. It was partly implemented on 6 December, when Governor Seitz, on a tour of the grassfields, separated Bangang and Babadju from Bali, and paid Fonyonga II 300 marks as compensation for lost influence.[38]

The separation of Bangang and Babadju opened the floodgates of independence throughout the realm. Real or imagined oppression by Bali became the most fashionable grievance of the day, as people sought to attract government sympathy by dramatising past and present practices of the Bali.

In the review of Bali activities that followed, a catalogue of grievances was assembled by the station, for which new remedies were proposed. This exercise gave the impression that the Bali domain was some repressive and corrupt set-up that was given to ever more repression and corruption. It was not remembered how that domain

38   *Memorandum of 11 September 1911*, from D.O. of Bamenda to the Governor.

had served German interests before. Or that the hated corvee was the main cause of the sub-town disaffection, Fonyonga oppressing them in order to keep up an excessive quota of forced labour for the plantations. And the Germans initially egged him on, arming his levies and giving him a free hand. But as the disaffection grew, they shifted their position.

Fonyonga was accused of arbitrarily distributing the head tax levied him, without due consideration for the population strength of the vassals, and much to the advantage of his immediate chiefdom. The vassal chiefs did not share in the stipend deriving therefrom, as Fonyonga delivered all the money to the station without stating what proportion came from the vassals and what came from Bali proper. He was accused of similar caprice in distributing his quota of labourers among the sub-towns, enlisting as much as half of the grown-up male population of some villages. And he was said to prevent the subject chiefs from lodging complaints at the station, harshly imprisoning any who tried. His "tădmànjì" were even more unpopular. They were accused of systematic oppression and extortion: exacting unpaid food supplies from the vassals under their control, frequently confiscating the best lands in those villages for their personal use, and sometimes forcibly taking away fields already cultivated.

The station duly put forward a series of remedial proposals. Henceforth, Fonyonga would have to specify the amount of tax from his vassals and share his stipend with their chiefs. He would also specify the proportion of labour recruited from the subject villages. The vassal chiefs were now permitted to bring their complaints directly to the station, and Fonyonga was prohibited from imprisoning any of them. Corrupt "tădmànjì" were to be dismissed, after returning farmlands illegally seized and paying for goods unlawfully exacted. And Fonyonga was to prohibit his people from wandering outside Bali itself.[39]

But the worst was yet to come. For no one scrutinised the Bali more closely than Governor Ebermaier, the most Baliphobic of the Germans. He saw the Bali as "misleading negro intriguers with a lust

---

39   *Report on Conditions in Bali Country*, Bamenda, 2 February 1912.

for power," and was convinced that the disaffection within the empire had no other cause than "the unreliable egotistical Bali policy," based on "egotistical negro diplomacy."[40] His appraisal of the Bali connection was as negative as his judgement of the Bali was harsh. As he told the German Colonial Office:

> Bali's importance as a supplier of labourers for the plantations on the Cameroon Mountain has for some time past been considerably on the wane, and in my opinion Fonyonga has proved himself utterly unsuitable as an intermediary between the political officers and the small tribes which still owe him allegiance. It is therefore high time that a determined policy of great reserve towards Bali should be followed.[41]

First, Bamumbu was freed, under the pretext that it was now part of the newly created Chang Division and that it was impossible to control an empire across divisional boundaries. Then Ebermaier decided to test the waters nearer home: in February 1912 Batibo was freed, its chief returned from exile and reinstated. When there was no protest from Fonyonga, the Governor proceeded with his programme.

On 6 December 1912, he summoned all the chiefs of what was left of the Bali sphere to a meeting at the Bamenda station. Announced as a meeting of coordination and information, it turned out to be an inquest into Bali rule, at which subject chiefs were encouraged to speak their minds. Then the Governor announced the new policy of the administration that "Every vassal enjoys the right to communicate directly with the station and to lodge his complaints there,"[42] without passing through the Fon of Bali. The Bamenda Declaration of 1912 was the penultimate nail in the coffin of the Bali Nyonga sphere of influence.

The final nail was the tax reforms of May 1914, which freed

---

40 *Dispatch by Governor Ebermaier*, Buea, 27 October 1912.
41 Ibid.
42 *Declaration by Governor Ebermaier at Meeting with Fonyonga II and his vassals*, Bamenda, 16 December 1912.

eighteen more subject villages from the Bali yoke:

1. Bamuwah	11. Bamessong
2. Bamunyi	12. Bakurabe
3. Bessi	13. Bamechom
4. Guzang	14. Pinyin
5. Bambo	15. Bamunung
6. Bamofa	16. Baforchu
7. Baba	17. Fongu [Babadju
8. Bangwa	18. Bamessinge
9. Bafomessang	
10. Mbatu	

These villages now received their tax tickets directly from the Germans and sent their returns straight to the station, receiving a 7% stipend in return. Although Fonyonga continued to receive 3% of their taxes as compensation for lost political power, the reforms marked the effective end of the Bali Nyonga sphere. Bali suzerainty was now restricted to the eleven Meta villages which had been forcibly resettled there in 1906.

The Bali were completely helpless as the Germans implemented the changes. For years, they had nibbled away at the powers of the Fon, so that when Ebermaier applied the final blow there was no strength left in him to resist. Fonyonga became a passive spectator at the funeral of his empire. The Germans had used the Bali to "pacify" the grassfields, and once that had been achieved, they needed police-men to keep the peace, not warriors to threaten it. So they turned to "pacifying" Bali itself, dismantling the empire in a way that would have embarrassed both Galega and Zintgraff. Kaberry and Chilver have absolved Fonyonga of any responsibility in this debacle, describing him as "the convenient scapegoat of a contradictory colonial policy,"[43] which sought to use him in a role of peace as an intermediary between the German administration and the chiefdoms of the south-western grassfields, and simultaneously in a role of war as a ruthless raider for

43   P.M. Kaberry and E.M. Chilver, "An Outline of the Traditional Political System of Bali Nyonga", p. 370.

ever-increasing quotas of forced labour for the plantations. And they expected him, like a chameleon, to change colour without incident.

The first Europeans left an indelible mark on the history of Bali Nyonga. Perceptions of their significance differed widely. Some say that the influence of Bali Nyonga was all of German making. Many Germans believed that too. True, they introduced the Bali to many activities in which they were not previously engaged. And they took the Bali to many places that they had never been before.

But there were few places in the Bamenda grassfields that had not known about the Bali before the arrival of the Germans. In fact, German penetration of those grassfields owed so much to the Bali that one is entitled to ask who served who? Yet the very idea of German penetration of the hinterland was incompatible with the existence of a powerful, independent Bali kingdom. So, the Germans gave the impression of supporting the Fon's power when, in reality, they were seeking to destroy that power and replace it with their own. When, with his help, the penetration was achieved, the Germans made a tremendous volte-face, and the Bali were punished for not paying sufficient attention to the small print of their history. Even the friend-liest German knew that Bali power was only a stepping stone towards their own ultimate power, a stepping stone that became an obstacle once the colonial administration was established. Ebermaier removed that obstacle with the cold anonymity of German officialdom. And so, the Bali Nyonga sphere of influence began its fatal decline with the arrival of the very first German.

SIX

Later Europeans
Bali Nyonga and the British

The dismemberment of the Bali empire was one of Ebermaier's last acts as German Governor of Kamerun, for while that was happening, the fever of war had gripped Europe, beginning a process of crisis and change from which Germany itself would emerge maimed and partitioned.

The European war of 1914-18 has been popularly called the First World War because although the bulk of the fighting took place in Europe, the war was soon exported overseas into the colonies of the feuding European countries, thereby converting much of the world into one vast theatre of war. Initially, the war pitted Germany and Austria-Hungary, known as the Central Powers, against an alliance of Britain, France and Russia, with each party progressively drawing in its own friends and allies. It was the first major war in Europe since Napoleon, and it was by far the costliest war in history in terms of human casualty. Its outbreak has been attributed basically to the failure of Europe to cope with the consolidated and industrial Germany which was making a belated but powerful bid for world power status.

As the war became increasingly atrocious and indiscriminate, German interests all over the world came under attack. The German colony of Kamerun was one such interest, especially as it was sandwiched between British Nigeria and French Equatorial Africa.

The Kamerun campaign of 1915 was the convergence of British and French troops from their neighbouring colonies to overrun the German colony, which they eventually partitioned among them.

The First World War and the Coming of the British

As the leading member of the Allied camp, Britain played a decisive role in the War, not only in Europe but overseas as well. The
Anglo-French expeditionary force in Kamerun was commanded by a
British officer, Major General Dobell, and it was his capture of Douala
in 1916 that signalled the end of German resistance in the territory.

But even before the final assault on Douala, the British had pen-
etrated well into the Bamenda grassfields, pressing hard after the
retreating Germans. Led by Major Crookenden, Commander of the
Cross River Column, they arrived Bali in the second half of October
1915. They used it as their base for the assault on Bamenda, which
they occupied on 22 October.

It appears that the arrival of the British was the subject of conflicting German advice to the Bali. As the German position deteriorated,
Von Sommerfeld advised Fonyonga II to remain neutral or even mildly
support the British, provide them with food and carriers and show
them the main roads of the grassfields, but not the bush paths.[1] This
latter reserve has encouraged the view that Von Sommerfeld was
using the Bali to trap the British, although nothing seemed to have
come from it.

However, Adametz and most of the staff of the station continued to
insist on the loyalty of Bali Nyonga to the German cause, arguing that
neutrality in the conflict was just as treasonable as opposition itself.[2]

But as the war developed, Fonyonga decided to support the British rather than the Germans. His reading of the situation convinced
him that the British had the best chance of victory. It is doubtful that
he could have acted otherwise. His relations with the Germans had
worsened as his empire disintegrated, and he had not forgiven them
for letting him down. Moreover, the German war situation seemed to
deteriorate by the day, and only a fool would have continued to stand
by them. So, the earlier German volte-face vis-a-vis the Bali made it
easier for Fonyonga to transfer his loyalty to the British.

Fonyonga received British troops, much as Galega had received

1   W.E. Hunt, *Assessment Report on the Bali Clan*, 1925, para. 30.
2   Ibid.

the Germans, giving them ample supplies of food, services and information that were to prove vital in the British offensive throughout the grassfields. The Bali did not only show them the main roads as Sommerfeld had recommended, they revealed all the footpaths and shortcuts, ravines and mountain passes, thereby neutralising the advantage of any knowledge of the terrain that the Germans might have acquired from years of occupation. Such was the decisive importance of Fonyonga's contribution to the British offensive that even before the war was over, the Fon of Bali Nyonga was presented with an autographed portrait of King George V as a token of gratitude from the British monarch.[3]

The estranged Germans were stung by what they regarded as a betrayal by an ally. They showed their anger in reprisal against Bali Nyonga. On 11 November 1915, having been tipped off by the chief of Baforchu that a lightly guarded British convoy of supplies had arrived Bali Nyonga, the Germans found reason to return there. Abramowski, who led the raid, reached Bali in the early hours of 12 November, brushed aside the make-shift local force hastily gathered by drum message, as well as the forty or so British soldiers who guarded the depot. After taking the British depot, the Germans stormed Fonyonga's palace, plundering it of goods and money worth some £2000, before setting it alight.[4]

The attack on Bali Nyonga demonstrated the growing paranoia of the Germans. Even the most optimistic of them knew that the Allied victory was only a matter of time. The fall of Douala to General Dobell effectively broke the German resistance. The tiny pockets of resistance that remained in the hinterland were gradually mobbed up. The eighteen-month campaign ended with Anglo-French occupation of Kamerun and the internment of the German forces, including Governor Ebermaier, in the neighbouring Spanish territory of Rio Muni.

But the Allies found the early administration of the occupied territory somewhat more difficult than its conquest had been. As the euphoria of victory died down, the ugly problems of running the

---

3   *Report on the Bali Patrol*, Bamenda, June 1920, paras. 4-5.
4   W.E. Hunt, op. cit.

territory emerged. The harmony that they had displayed during the war was not forthcoming in peacetime. General Dobell was much criticised by the French for alleged partiality in running the territory occupied by the joint force. Not that anyone would have found such a task easy or thankful. He did not receive much sympathy from the locals either. The Germans had planted mines of disobedience among the native people, warning them that any collaboration with the British and French would be most severely punished when they returned to the territory. So, at first the natives were sceptical of the new white men as the ghosts of the old ones continued to haunt the land.

This situation was not helped by uncertainty over the future of the territory. As criticism of Dobell mounted, the French proposed the establishment of a "carefully balanced" Franco-British condominium over the territory, pending the conclusion of peace in Europe.[5] This condominium would give the French an equal share in the administration of the territory, if nothing else. But the British turned down the idea, arguing that it would "inevitably give rise to difficulties and probably to friction between the two countries."[6] Instead, they proposed the provisional division of the territory into two administrative spheres under their respective governments.[7] In other words, the British proposed the partition of Kamerun in lieu of the condominium suggested by France. The latter agreed to the partition, with firm ideas about its share of the bargain. At a meeting in London on 24 February 1916, the French delegate, Georges Picot, produced a map showing that the whole of Kamerun was desired by France, with the exception of a tiny strip of territory along the south-eastern border of Nigeria.[8]

After consultations with the War Committee, the British delegation unexpectedly accepted the French proposals, demanding only marginal concessions, notably, that the portion of the Bornu empire lying to the east of the Nigerian border, that is, the north-western tip of Kamerun, should be administered by the United Kingdom.[9] The

5   British Foreign Office Records, F.O./7086 Sec., of 6/2/1915.
6   F.O./3577 of 22/1/1916.
7   F.O./7533 of 16/2/1916.
8   British Colonial Office Records, Letter N° 35941 of 24/2/1916.
9   F.O./9156/16 of 26/2/1916.

French gleefully obliged, and the deal was concluded on 3 March 1916 and formalised in the Franco-British Declaration on the Cameroons of 10 July 1919. Commenting on the gross inequality in the sizes of their respective spheres of the former Kamerun, the British Colonial Secretary pointed out that his Government's approach to the partition was based rather on "considerations affecting British relations with the French which have no connection with the respective shares which have been taken by the two nations in the conquest of the Cameroons."[10] In other words, the disproportion between the war effort in Kamerun and the share of the booty had to do with a wider perspective of Anglo-French relations: France had borne the brunt of the German onslaught in Europe and was thought to need some compensation overseas.

The partition of the German Kamerun put the Bamenda grassfields into the British Cameroons, separating it almost clinically from the Bamileke and Bamun grassfields which were carved into the French sector. The people of these grassfields braced themselves for the impending changes with some trepidation: they were getting used to the Germans when the War came, a war in which they knew neither head nor tail, and now they welcomed the British, not knowing whether the Germans had gone for good. Amid all the uncertainty, however, Bali Nyonga was more hopeful than most: having fallen out with the Germans, they looked forward to making a fresh start with the British.

Bali Nyonga under British Rule

British rule was formally established in the Bamenda grassfields in January 1916 when Podevin took over as the first D.O. of Bamenda Division. As had been the case with the Germans before them, the first British administrators were very impressed by the Bali, partly out of gratitude for their support during the war but also from their own independent judgement. Many had thought and some had hoped that the Bali would be stigmatised in the eyes of the British for their

---

10   *Telegram to the Governor-General of Nigeria*, in F.O./9999/16 of 1/3/1916.

crucial role in setting up the German power base in the Bamenda grassfields. But the German relationship had been so short and had turned so sour towards the end that the Bali were able to claim the new friendship without any apologies for their past. The British on the other hand seemed pleased with the strategic location of Bali Nyonga, the efficient organisation of its society and the eager expeditiousness of the people. Podevin noted that Bali was "far and away the most advanced of the various tribal divisions" in the Bamenda grassfields and that Fonyonga was a really powerful man.[11] While N.C. Duncan, who replaced him as D.O., was literally charmed by the personality of the Fon, describing him after only their first meeting as "the most intelligent and far-seeing native gentleman whom I have encountered during eighteen years spent in West and South Africa."[12]

And such indeed was Fonyonga's aura that the British were puzzled by running arguments over the existence and extent of Bali Nyonga suzerainty. To separate fact from fiction the British commissioned several inquiries. W.E. Hunt, who led one of the most exhaustive inquiries, confessed that,

> I had at first thought that Bali's power had been exaggerated and that she owed her authority largely to the Germans; but the more information I collect the more I come to the conclusion that the Bali's suzerainty extended over a larger area before the Germans came than after and the Germans gradually reduced the (Fon's) sphere of influence.[13]

Even so, the beginnings of British rule were rather heady days in Bali Nyonga. The War had brought about a major upheaval within the kingdom, as one after another of the remaining vassals rebelled against Fonyonga and declared themselves independent. The revolt began late in 1915 when the chiefs of Bambunji, Bamenjong and Bamyensi abandoned their new settlements within Bali and ran away into the

---

11 *Bamenda Divisional Report, 1917.*
12 *Report on the Bali Patrol, Bamenda, June 1920, para. 4.*
13 *Report Supplementary to the Bamenda Divisional Report for 1920.*

hills and swamps where they were joined by their followers.

The causes of the revolt are varied. It is believed by some to have been orchestrated by chief Fongang of Guzang who had a personal feud with Fonyonga and wanted to poach the Meta vassals to swell his own ranks.[14] But many think that the upheaval was the product of the change of German attitude towards Bali. This is thought to have worked in many ways. First, the vassals held the Germans responsible for their presence in Bali, having brought them there. So, when the Germans left, they thought they might return to their former homes. Secondly, the vassals felt that the Germans were the mainstay of Bali power, so when the very Germans turned against Fonyonga to the point of burning his palace, the sub-towns could not detect a better signal to throw off the Bali yoke. Yet another view suggests that the revolt of the vassals was actually incited by the angry Germans as punishment for Fonyonga's disloyalty during the War. The British later discovered that the Germans had distributed rifles to the villages concerned to arm their rebellion.[15]

Fonyonga's reaction to the revolt showed how much his position had shifted over the issue of Meta resettlement within Bali. He had been hostile to the plan when it was launched in 1906, failing to see the sense in resettling some of his subjects within the empire. But as that empire disintegrated under the impact of new German laws, Fonyonga found himself clinging to the resettled vassals as the last vestiges of a once mighty realm. He could not condone their departure from Bali, as that meant his loss of control over them.

Neither did the British. Out of gratitude to the Fon for his willing assistance during the War, they felt obliged to quell any rebellion against him. So, when the three vassal villages ran away in October 1915, Major Crookenden, who commanded British troops in Bamenda, promptly brought them back to Bali and assured Fonyonga that no further breakaways would be tolerated by the British administration.

However, Crookenden and Fonyonga did not reckon with the determination of the vassals to gain their freedom. They soon ran

14   W. E. Hunt, *Confidential Report* E.22/1920 of 15/12/1920.
15   *Report on the Bali Patrol, Bamenda,* June 1920, para. 6-7.

away again, this time followed by Batabi and Banja. And still the British, under Fonyonga's urging, were adamant. In January 1916 when Podevin took over the civil charge of Bamenda Division, he decided that the authority of the Fon of Bali over the runaway chiefs must be restored. In March 1916 he dispatched a patrol of fifty British soldiers, commanded by Captain Armstrong, to enforce their return to Bali. Their new villages in the hills were stormed, their crops and houses destroyed. But they refused to return to Bali, escaping further into the forest. In the end, the patrol returned to Bamenda, having failed in its mission.

A second patrol under N.C. Duncan, the new D.O. of Bamenda, with two companies commanded by Captain Vertue and Captain Mulock, went out in March 1920 for the same purpose. They adopted the same strategy as the first patrol - and they obtained the same results, as the vassals fled, leaving no one to be brought back to Bali.

In between the patrols, both sides in the drama engaged in a flurry of diplomatic activity to woo the British to their cause. Fonyonga II continued to pay taxes for the five runaway villages out of his pocket. While the villages themselves sent several envoys to the station offering to pay tax and obey the government in every respect, provided that Fonyonga's overlordship over them was rescinded.

The determined Meta resistance, coupled with their declared willingness to cooperate directly with the government, convinced the administration to open an inquiry into the exact nature of the relationship between Fonyonga and the vassals. The six-month investigation was conducted by W.E. Hunt, the new D.O. of Bamenda. Mr Hunt conceded in his report that "there was no sound case for coercion [of the runaway vassals back to Bali] because Britain would not have approved of the initial German policy of driving the Menemos into Bali."[16] Commenting on that report, the Lieutenant Governor observed in similar view that "Even if in the days prior to German occupation these villages did recognize the suzerainty of the Fon of Bali, the action of the German Government in compelling the villages to come and

---

16   W. E. Hunt, *Confidential Report* N° C2/21 of 10/6/21.

live in Bali caused the keenest resentment."[17]

The crisis confronted the British with a serious dilemma. The runaway sub-towns were bent on not returning to Bali. After failing twice, the British were reluctant to bring down their full military might against five tiny villages that had done no other wrong than return to their original homes. On the other hand, the Bali were looking to the British to live up to their commitment towards the integrity of their kingdom. The situation was further complicated by the prospect of widespread traditional upheaval inherent in freeing the runaway vassals, as the Lieutenant Governor pointed out:

> It is more probable that other villages will break away from Bali if these villages are not compelled to acknowledge its suzerainty and it is also possible that the general movement by certain sub-chiefs to disown the overlordship of their proper and recognized Head Chiefs will receive such encouragement.[18]

On balance, however, the British felt that their own integrity would be enhanced if they were seen to depart from activities that had any resemblance with the arbitrary practices of the Germans. It was this image of justice and fairness that they wanted to portray to the people of the Cameroons, and they could not begin by endorsing the policies of the Germans. So, they leaned on Fonyonga to give up the runaway villages as well as any others which had been forced into Bali by the Germans but now wished to return to their original homes.

The offer was eagerly accepted by the remaining villages, except Bossa which was situated so close to Bali that it risked losing all its land were it to leave. The fact that it chose to remain meant that living in Bali was not as bad as the other protesting villages made it seem. But rather than split hairs over maintaining Bali suzerainty, the British pressed ahead with the independence of the sub-towns. They suspended the 3% stipend due to Fonyonga on taxes from the Menemo

---

17   *Confidential Memorandum on the Bali Area, Bamenda*, 3/10/1921.
18   Ibid.

villages, in exchange for a consolidated annual subsidy of £120,[19] thereby bringing what was left of the Bali empire to a formal end. In freeing the remaining sub-towns, however, the Lieutenant Governor, ruled that: "the freed villages can have no claim to the land in Bali on which they lived and farmed during their compulsory detention and which they have now vacated."[20] The pertinence of that ruling did not come to light until 30 years later, when a new upheaval engulfed Bali and its Meta neighbours over the land in question.

For the time being, the British advanced the dismemberment of the Bali sphere of influence initiated by the Germans. By 1924 Bali Nyonga had been reduced to its heartland of old settlement and early assimilation. All the trappings of empire had been lost. Yet amid the gloom of losing all but one of the Bali sub-towns, W.E. Hunt spotted one glimmer of hope for Fonyonga II: now the Fon of Bali could turn his attention to the development of his kingdom rather than in endless arguments over land and power.[21]

Indications are that Fonyonga accepted his losses with good grace and indeed turned his attention to improving what was left of a once-mighty sphere.

In the first decade of British rule, Bali Nyonga adapted to the new system of local government that the British introduced in the territory. The centrepiece of that new system was the creation of Native Authorities by which village communities within the same geographical area or with a similar cultural background were brought together to carry out their own local administration and thrash out local problems. The British duly created a Native Authority in Bali Nyonga, which also covered Bali Gham.

Bali Nyonga was one of the most dynamic Native Authorities in the Bamenda grassfields, one that was both a pilot and a pivot of the new system, in which the British tried many administrative experiments. In 1923 the British opened the first Native Authority school in the Bamenda grassfields in Bali Nyonga. This was followed by the

---

19   W.E. Hunt, *Confidential Report N° C2/21 for 10/6/1921*.
20   *Confidential Memorandum on the Bali Area, Bamenda*, 3/10/1921, p. 6.
21   *Supplement to the Bamenda Divisional Report for 1921*.

native court in April 1925. And later the same year, the road from Bali Nyonga to Bamenda was opened. Fonyonga II was so thrilled with the new road that he bought bicycles for all his principal courtiers.[22]

The coming of the British was thus a question of continuity and change for the Bali. For many in the grassfields, the departure of the Germans went unnoticed, despite the War, and the British were just another group of white men. But for the Bali Nyonga, the British brought changes that could only have been dreamt about in earlier years. They arranged the burial of the Bali empire without conducting a proper post-mortem. Then they helped the Bali navigate what might otherwise have been a traumatic transition, from a quasi-feudal empire to a modern kingdom.

Bali Nyonga embraced the new administration, working its way back to the forefront of development in the Bamenda grassfields. And although the cushion of the empire was gone, Bali Nyonga remained the centre of an expanding web of relationships throughout the grassfields. Its weekly market attracted the most business, some from as far as the coast. The first college in the grassfields [Basel Mission College], opened there in 1949; the first airstrip a few years later. And in their general demeanour, natives of Bali radiated ease and self-assurance, even though the ghost of the past continued to stalk them.

22   G.V. Evans, *Bamenda Divisional Report for 1925.*

SEVEN

Assault on the Fondom
The Riots of 1952

Fonyonga II felt the cuts and bruises of Bali Nyonga more than anyone else. Although the British tried to minimise the point, the eventual disappearance of Bali suzerainty broke the Fon's heart. He was distressed to see his inheritance whittling away before his own eyes. His agony was exacerbated by the fact that he could not do anything about it. And he never forgave the colonial administration for making it impossible for a man to claim his due. As the frustration mounted, Fonyonga's health began to fail. In March 1928 he fell so seriously ill that many thought the end had come. But it had not. As the fighter that he was, he not only recovered but hung on for another twelve years. When he finally died on 29 August 1940, few could be thought to have lived a fuller life, in terms of age as well as incident.

Fonyonga's passing turned a new leaf in Bali history, for he had so fully incarnated the empire that towards the end, his own life became something of an anachronism. With the loss of the empire, Bali needed a different figure to breathe fresh life into the new era. They found one in Prince Vincent Samdala, who was enthroned on 3 September 1940 as Galega II.

The Coming of Galega II

Galega II was a king of the new age. Unlike his predecessors, he had prepared for leadership, not on the fields of battle but in the corridors of a dispensary, tending the sick and giving hope to the distressed. His general outlook was therefore one of peace, an outlook enhanced by his education and travel. Moreover, he came to the throne without being too closely linked with the events of the past. Unlike Fonyonga II who, as Tita Gwenjang, had played a significant role in building the empire that he later inherited, Galega II had no direct responsibility in the demise of that empire. Much as he deeply regretted it, he was not personally accountable for the loss. He thus began his reign without the inhibitions that the numerous traumas of the past would have had on someone closely associated with it.

After seeing off an unexpected challenge to his succession from Tita Nyambi, Galega II went to work to improve the kingdom that he had inherited. His first priority was to bring stability to that kingdom. He was dismayed to learn that Bali had very few genuine friends. It had so terrorised the neighbourhood that it had precious few allies. In a persistent peace initiative, Galega set out to make amends, extending a hand of friendship to his peers throughout the grassfields. Many responded favourably, but the one that stood out in Galega's memory was the remarkable relationship that he forged with Sultan Njoya of the Bamun.[1] It all started as a tentative gift-exchange relationship, and then developed into a booming friendship in which both rulers visited each other frequently and consulted on a broad range of issues.

Notwithstanding his desire for change, Galega was exceedingly proud of the history of his people, so much so that he set up a committee of elders to reconstruct, document and preserve it. An early act of his reign would be the most significant: with an eye on the future, he welcomed the idea of the missionaries to open a college in his fondom, offering them vast expanses of land in 1949 for that purpose. And Basel Mission College, Bali, which was to be one of the signature realisations of his era, was the pioneer college throughout the grassfields.

Galega II was among the first traditional rulers to realise that the tribe was no longer the focus of human relations, as the fate of the territory as a whole became a matter of common interest. He joined the bandwagon of national politics, becoming an eminent political

---

1   Interview with VS. Galega II, Bali, 20/8/84.

figure in the British Cameroons, as Vice President of the House of Chiefs. He actively participated at various conferences that were held to discuss the future of the territory, using his traditional aura to bring stability and conciliation to the proceedings.

While dabbling in politics, however, Galega II did not compromise his integrity as a traditional ruler. In fact, his stature never stopped growing. He had such an immense personality that his presence literally filled every audience. He spoke softly, forcing the audience to listen, which added to the mystique. Yet on public occasions, he became so vibrant and fleet-footed that age seemed to simply bounce off him. What was more, he thoroughly enjoyed his responsibilities, basking in the veneration of his people and making light work of what was indeed a heavy burden. He aroused and sustained the interest of the people in the chieftaincy more than anyone before him. His every public appearance was carefully choreographed, with the people yearning to see more of him every time. And like an accomplished performer, he usually gave them just enough presence to retain their appetite for the next occasion. In his reign, the chieftaincy became one of Bali Nyonga's sacred institutions, a rallying point par excellence.

But the aura of Galega's office was achieved at the expense of the efficient administration of the realm. The seclusion of that office meant that the Fon was not a hands-on administrator, relying instead on attendants and advisers to resolve the critical issues of governance. Not once, he fell foul to the whims of unscrupulous servants, who carried out unpopular personal vendettas in his name!

Still, these were only minor hiccups in Galega's long reign. By far his greatest challenge was the relationship of Bali Nyonga with its neighbours. He had no illusions about it. But he was surprised by the intractable nature of the bitterness towards his people. And he did not anticipate that Bali-Meta relations would become such healthy breeding ground for agitators. Yet many a man has eaten a square meal in life by simply stroking the unease to the appropriate audience.

The heart of the matter was ownership of the land that fell vacant following the release of ten of the eleven Meta villages that the Germans had forced into Bali in 1909. And to pre-empt any prospective dispute, the British Lieutenant Governor had ruled that "The [freed

Meta] villages can have no claim to the land in Bali on which they lived and farmed during their compulsory detention in Bali and which they have now vacated."[2]

But as the dust settled on that emphatic ruling, dissatisfied Meta tribesmen constantly revisited the substance of the question, probing and searching for new answers. The Widikum riot of 1952 in which this long protest culminated was the turning point of Bali-Meta relations, and the defining event of Galega's reign.

Background to the Unrest

The Widikum riot seemed destined to occur at some point in the history of their relationship with Bali. It was almost in the natural order of things for the Widikum to rise up one day against those who exercised suzerainty over them.

Incidentally, some of the seeds of this revolt were sown by the Bali themselves. Their style of conquest seemed less definite and left much room for doubt and reversal. Unlike the Bamun who dispersed conquered peoples after seizing their lands, the Bali treated their conquests with respect. They reasoned that Bali suzerainty would be more palatable if it were presented in a more civilised manner. In that way, conquered peoples would be more apt to collaborate with the Bali out of their own free will. So, the Bali did not persecute the "niwəmbè." They did not seize their lands. Instead, they allowed most of the conquered peoples to stay on their lands, even those very close to Bali itself, provided they accepted Bali suzerainty over them. In so doing there was a mathematical adjustment of frontiers whereby the boundaries of Bali now included the conquered villages. Technically, these villages were now living within Bali, on what by dint of conquest had become Bali land. But in practice no real change of domicile had occurred, and many of the "niwəmbè" continued to think of their village as it had been before. Moreover, the fact that these conquered communities were maintained as whole units, albeit within Bali, increased their chances of one day rising against their conquerors, and it facilitated

2 *Confidential Memorandum on the Bali Area*, Bamenda, 3/9/21, p. 6.

the task of freeing them. Ironically, then, the fact that Bali conquest was less ruthless than it might have been acted as a major catalyst in later Meta uprisings against them.

However, in freeing the sub-towns which had become incorporated into Bali proper, a new complication arose: the people could not be freed without land. By the Bali conquest they had been dispossessed of their land and continued to live on it only by the grace of their conquerors.

But to many, this difference was only apparent. Most of the sub-towns regarded their freedom as a theoretical exercise, involving no physical movement except that the Bali boundary would be so retracted that they would thenceforth be outside Bali. Needless to say, that the Bali found such an arrangement totally unacceptable. So, the independence of those sub-towns incorporated in Bali invariably created a land dispute within Bali.

The first of these disputes involved Baforchu. Freed by the Germans in 1914, it had immediately laid claim to the land it had been occupying as an incorporated sub-town of Bali, a claim strongly denied by the Fon of Bali. Unfortunately, the First World War overshadowed the ensuing dispute and after the War the British took time to settle down before addressing it. They eventually did so on 26 February 1923, in a ruling that brought mixed blessings to the Baforchu: The British Government upheld their independence from Bali, but rejected their claim to the land in dispute, taking the view that the land had become Bali land through conquest. Mr. G.V. Evans, later D.O. of Bamenda Division, hailed the ruling, saying that "this long drawn out and contentious problem so admirably handled by Mr. Hunt, D.O., and tactfully carried into effect by Mr. Hawkesworth, has at last reached a successful conclusion."[3]

The Baforchu ruling momentarily discouraged other incorporated sub-towns from seeking their own freedom and from claiming the land in Bali on which they had been resettled. But there was no doubt that if and when the political climate changed, they would.

---

3 G.V. Evans, *Annual Report for Bamenda Division*, 1923.

The nature of the Bali settlement was also a source of conflict: it was heavily concentrated in a core area, with the outlying lands reserved for farming and grazing. This type of settlement had obvious military advantages: in case of emergency, the entire army could be mobilised at short notice. While in peacetime the concentration strengthened social and cultural bonding among the constituent groups, a process from which a distinct Bali culture was emerging.

But in peace as in war, the settlement had serious shortcomings. The high concentration in the centre meant that the outlying areas were open to infiltration, a fatal prospect for a people obsessed with their security. But most importantly perhaps, the apparent emptiness of the outlying areas gave the impression, not least to the Meta, that Bali had more land than it actually needed. Yet, if the Bali were to live in the sort of consolidated settlement that was typical of many grassfields peoples, where every family lived alone on its entire farmland, in other words, if the Bali were not so security conscious as to all want to nestle together, one might have found it difficult to escape the conclusion that in reality Bali Nyonga needed more land than it actually had. Unfortunately, this was not obvious, even though the population density in Bali was so much higher than everywhere in the Bamenda grassfields. The irony of Bali settlement was that although there was hardly a yard between some houses in the centre, one could wander for miles in the farmlands of the outskirts without meeting a single house. The result was the impression that the Bali greedily arrogated lands that they did not genuinely need. It was such lands that the Meta wanted to claim.

History contributed handsomely to the Meta uprising, and every twist of fate was interpreted as an omen for the downfall of Bali. The Meta watched with bated breath as the relationship between Bali and the Germans deteriorated. Then they jumped at the opportunity of German incitement to rise against their conquerors. In their duplicity, the Germans now convinced the Meta that the Bali had unlawfully occupied their lands and that they themselves had been misled into supporting a vicious expansionist scheme which ought to have been resisted from the start. Not that the Germans were strangers at changing their minds. Or that they needed to believe themselves all the time.

But on their way out, they decided to leave their successors with as much confusion as possible, creating as many pockets of discontent as the time available could permit. In this respect therefore, the Meta uprising against the Bali might be interpreted as an aspect of German strategy in the War against the Allied Powers.

At the beginning the British did little against the resurgence of Baliphobia among some of the Meta. They were, understandably, more concerned with securing total victory over the Germans. And when that was done, they did not wish to rush into any alliances, even though they were clearly appalled by several aspects of the German administration of the Bamenda grassfields. Yet the fact that they did not immediately side with Bali as the Germans had done on arrival, preferring instead a more considered and even-handed approach, convinced the Meta that Fonyonga's luck had finally run out.

The Legal Impasse

British abhorrence of some German practices did not mean that they would deploy arbitrary techniques to bring such practices to an end. That would have made them just another bunch of Germans. Instead, they were interested in instituting the rule of law, not maintaining the rule of luck. So, when the people of Bamungen [Mungen Mbu] took up the Widikum challenge against Bali, they came before a British administration that would not be swayed by sentiment.

The Bamungen had cleverly allowed dust to settle on the Baforchu ruling of February 1923. After fifteen years, they reasoned that the essence of that ruling would have been forgotten. Even more cleverly, they now presented their problem not as an outright claim for land, which had been definitively quashed in the Baforchu ruling, but as a simple boundary dispute with Bali. And they scored an initial victory when Mr. F.A. Goodliffe, Senior District Officer for Bamenda, was appointed to hold an inquiry with a view to determining the disputed boundary between Bali and Bamungen.

That was as far as their luck ran. The inquiry unearthed the famous 1923 ruling, which Mr. Goodliffe felt bound to reiterate, concluding that "The Mungen Mbu people had lost all their rights over the land in dispute to the Bali people who had acquired it from them by conquest sometime before 1890 and, therefore, it was not possible to fix a boundary between them."[4]

But the Bamungen were not deterred. They applied to the Chief Commissioner to review Goodliffe's decision. After careful study, the Commissioner upheld the decision, stating that there were no merits in the Bamungen appeal. He intimated nonetheless that they could institute legal proceedings for a declaration of title on the disputed land.[5]

This legal recourse was gratefully accepted by the estranged Bamungen. In 1950 they commenced a series of actions in the Bali Native Court against the Fon of Bali, which were later transferred to the Supreme Court of Nigeria, Calabar Judiciary Division.[6] They also convinced eight other Widikum villages surrounding Bali to institute similar actions against the Fon of Bali.[7] The Bali-Widikum crisis of 1950-1952 had begun. It moved on swiftly, from drama in the courtroom to violence on the land.

The courtroom episode concerned the consolidated Meta suits against Bali, in which they claimed a declaration of title to large portions of Bali land, which they referred to as "Tadkon-Widikum Tribe Land," damages worth £10,000 [ten thousand pounds sterling] for trespass, and an injunction prohibiting the Bali from entering the disputed lands. The case came up for hearing on 25 February 1952, and immediately collapsed on a simple technicality: the Supreme Court non-suited the plaintiffs for not pleading title to the land in dispute, and that without such a title their claim for damages and an injunction could not be entertained. Mr. Justice Palmer who adjudicated then awarded £150 [one hundred and fifty pounds] in costs to the Bali defendants. What was more, the Widikum were further informed by the Court that the title in question could only be granted by the Governor.

They were perplexed and aggrieved. The Commissioner for the Cameroons, whom they regarded as the Governor, had advised them

---

4 *Nigeria Gazette Extraordinary,* N° 37, Vol. 40, Lagos, 8/8/53 pp. 577-578.
5 Ibid.
6 Supreme Court of Nigeria, Calabar Judicial Division, *Suit* N° C/33/1950.
7 *Suits* N° C/55/50, C/64/50, and C/65/50.

to pursue their claim to a declaration of title in the Supreme Court. Then the Court dismissed their claim for not pleading the title for which they had gone to court in the first place. It was a chicken-and-egg situation that completely bewildered them: the Governor told them to go to Court and the Court told them to go to the Governor. They were left in the middle.

This sudden termination, with heavy costs, of their Supreme Court suits imposed too heavy a strain on the patience of the Meta villages concerned. A few days later they vented their anger by invading Bali territory, causing widespread damage to property.

Attacks on the Realm

The Widikum uprising of 3 March 1952 did not look like a spontaneous riot. It is even doubtful that it was a direct reaction to the Palmer Judgement. Frederick Goodliffe who was Acting Resident in Bamenda at the time maintains that there would still have been a war, irrespective of the Judgement.[8] Communications in the territory were so poor that in the week that elapsed before the attack, news of the Judgement might not have reached some of the Meta villages that took part in the uprising. Indications are that it was a pre-conceived insurrection, timed to coincide with the Supreme Court hearing, which was anticipated to deliver a favourable ruling, giving them right to recover the lands in dispute.

The intensity of the uprising was terrifying. For a whole week, beginning on 3 March 1952, the Widikum villages surrounding Bali simply went on the rampage. Armed with dane guns, spears and matchets, they waged war on Bali land and property, looting and burning and destroying at random.

The riot claimed fifteen lives, four of which were Bali, and destroyed property on a scale unseen before. An official assessment of the damage found that 1520 dwelling houses and 370 store houses belonging to the Bali were burnt down. The Meta, mainly those living in the mixed settlements of Mungen Muwa, Mungen Mbu and Bossa,

8   *The Bali-Widikum Riots, 1952, Letter from the Acting Resident* N° C77/2 of 7 March 1952.

lost 130 dwelling houses and 20 store houses. A conservative estimate of the damage was put at £8000, to say nothing of the loss of livestock and the damage to crops and economic trees which was impossible to assess, but which in the opinion of the Commission of Inquiry "would amount to a substantial sum."[9]

Aftermath of the Crisis

The uprising took the Bali completely unawares, although in the end they coped with the situation to the best of their ability. They lost more property, even if they suffered fewer casualties.

The Government too had been most unprepared for the crisis. In spite of Goodliffe's forewarning that war was imminent regardless of the judgement of the Supreme Court on the land dispute, Government troops did not arrive the area until after several crucial days. And although the law came down mercilessly on the agitators -- 56 natives of Meta were subsequently convicted of offenses directly connected to the riot -- this delay was largely to blame for much of the damage caused on property. In the end the Government felt obliged to conduct a thorough post-mortem of the crisis. On 18 March 1952, the Governor duly appointed a Commission of Inquiry, composed of the eminent Mr. Justice A.G.B. Manson as sole Commissioner, to look into the matter.

After an exhaustive inquiry lasting nearly three months, Justice Manson reported that the uprising had nothing spontaneous about it: "There can be little doubt," he said, "that they [the Widikum] were encouraged, if not instigated and indeed organized by their leaders."[10]

On the substantive issues of the Widikum claim, the learned Commissioner was categorical: "the Widikum claims of occupational rights over the area in dispute cannot be entertained as there are no grounds either legal or equitable or compassionate which justify any such rights being granted to them."[11] Neither did he have any sympathy whatsoever for the plea "ad misericordiam" lodged by the Widikum

9   *Nigeria Gazette*, N° 45, Vol. 39, Lagos, 26 August 1952.
10   *Nigeria Gazette Extraordinary*, N° 37, Vol. 40 of 8 August 1953, pp. 577-578.
11   Ibid., p. 584.

leadership. He dismissed their complaints of hardship, deprivations and illegal Bali exactions as having no foundation whatever. As far as he was concerned, "Their alleged sufferings are a figment of their imagination if, indeed, they have not been disingenuously concocted to support their claim."[12]

Mr. Justice Manson could not understand why the Bali should be expected to give any portion of their land to those Widikum who had chosen to leave Bali. Neither could the chief of Ngwo, one of the Meta villages, who pointedly asked, "would anyone give a shovel to a wife who has decided to leave him and find a new husband?"[13]

The situation seemed so obvious that it was some wonder for the case to have been brought. But there was no telling what a corrupt and self-seeking leadership could attempt. Some had elevated Baliphobia into a political crusade. As the Commission of Inquiry noted:

> The Widikum communities have been ill-advised, misguided and misled by unscrupulous agitators who have, for personal motives, persuaded the great majority of the simple Widikum people to contribute out of their slender means their small subscriptions of a shilling or two towards the financing of litigation which is merely a speculative gamble and known to be such by those who have taken a principal part in instituting it.[14]

Justice Manson had arrived at this conclusion because he had discovered in the course of his inquiry that but for these agitators who thrived on causing discord among men, there would be no serious problem between the Bali and the Widikum living in Bali. As a matter of fact, he had found overwhelming evidence to show that,

> Widikum people on Bali land are accepted by the Bali as citizens having equal rights. They have intermarried, they

12   Ibid., p. 582.
13   Ibid.
14   Ibid., p. 584.

attend the same schools at Bali Nyonga, they are permitted to choose their own Quarter or Village Head, and there is no reliable evidence to show that they are not permitted freely to perform their own customs and religious ceremonies without interference by the Bali.[15]

So, the Commissioner urged the Government to watch out for saboteurs and polemists who were mounting innocent Widikum people against the Bali and seeking to create a crisis that they would then exploit for selfish political purposes. There was doubtless a group of men strongly opposed to all forms of Bali-Widikum rapprochement, who sought instead to open the old wounds that time had healed, to cause drama, sensation and controversy, and in so doing fabricate a cause to champion.

Mr Justice Manson could not hide his contempt for the agitators, concluding that:

> the acceptance by Government of the claims of the Widikum people either in whole or in part, will be regarded by them and others not only as an example of what may be gained by persistent petitioning and propaganda but also to some extent, as a condonation of, if not justification for, the recent disturbances which were created by the Widikum people.[16]

The Government endorsed the Commissioner's finding as to Bali ownership of the land in dispute, thereby conclusively rejecting the Widikum claim for portions of that land. As penalty for the riot, a fine of £10,000 was imposed on all indigenous inhabitants of the Moghamo group area, the Meta clan area and the Ngemba court area who had taken part in the uprising. Of that fine, £9,000 was to be applied in compensation to the Bali for injuries caused to them by the disturbances.[17] That compensation was put to collective use in the form of

---

15   Ibid., p. 583.
16   Ibid., pp. 585-586.
17   *Supplement to the Nigeria Gazette Extraordinary*, N° 45, Vol. 39, Part B, Lagos,

potable water supply for the entire chiefdom. As for the future, the Government decided that any boundary adjustment between Bali and its Widikum neighbours in favour of the latter could only be done with the express approval of the Bali and upon adequate compensation for any lands lost.[18]

Considering the scale of the damage from the riot, the compensation paid to the Bali was only a token. Of more importance perhaps was the ruling of the Government, which they regarded as a significant moral victory. It was now clear that the Widikum claim for portions of Bali land could not be entertained. This claim itself was quite absurd, for the Bamenda grassfields in the eighteenth and early nineteenth centuries was a region in such constant mutation, characterised by such rapid succession of states that it was virtually impossible to establish the original owners of any land. Moreover, such hair-splitting exercise would have invited a tremendous upheaval of claim and counterclaim that could lead to nothing but chaos. To be sure, the Widikum had no logical claim to the land in dispute, having themselves migrated from Tadkon not long before the first Chamba raids, and having been only forcefully resettled by the Germans on the land which they now claimed.

The Bali Nyonga leadership was tempered by the events of March 1952. The administration had urged them not to retaliate, for fear of creating a conflagration that might spiral out of control. So, they looked on as their properties went up in flames. It was a most peculiar situation for a people with their record in war. But the flames also consumed years of progress in Bali-Widikum rapprochement. In the crisis, there was both good news and bad news. The good news was that the riot had not been a spontaneous tribal uprising reflecting a deep-seated animosity between the Widikum and the Bali. Both communities had since come to terms with the fact of having to live side by side, even intermarrying and exchanging cultural activities. On the contrary, the riot had been organised by insurgent agents who deceived innocent Widikum people to take part in a gamble

26 August 1952.
18   *Nigeria Gazette Extraordinary*, N° 37, Vol. 40, Lagos, 8 June 1953, p. 587.

whose success might have brought glory to the organisers, but whose failure brought misery to the whole tribe. The bad news was that those agitators were not finished; they were likely to reappear under different cover. Going forward, their existence cast a somber shadow over Bali-Widikum relations.

The Bali Nyonga did not dwell on the frustrations of 1952. The rebuilding of the village began almost immediately. It was slower than the destruction had been. But the adversity of the crisis strengthened the spirit of togetherness among the people. The whole of Bali Nyonga became one community building site, as a new village was raised from the rubble of the old, in song and chatter.

The 1952 crisis also increased government sympathy towards Bali Nyonga. Administrative officials visited more often than before, trying to make up for failing to prevent the uprising. And on 27 May 1955, Galega II hosted the inauguration of the Bali airport, the first such facility in the Bamenda grassfields. The day was significantly symbolic: the people who had introduced the horse in those grassfields now witnessed the arrival of the very first aeroplane. The sight was comparable only with the coming of the first European six decades earlier. It was the dawn of a new day in Bali Nyonga.

EIGHT

Bali Nyonga Since Independence

The new era was characterised by the quest for self-determination across Africa. Everywhere on the continent, budding national elites rose to replace departing European administrators. The Europeans departed reluctantly, some grudgingly, and some only symbolically.

In the British Cameroons the new era was a period of excitement and uncertainty, but also of friction and fracture. After a spirited campaign in 1961, the people voted in a plebiscite to go in different directions. While the Southern Cameroons opted to unite with the French-speaking Cameroun Republic, the Northern Cameroons chose to remain in Nigeria. The Bali Chamba also went in different directions: Bali Muti which was found in the Northern Cameroons remained in Nigeria, while Bali Nyonga, Bali Kumbat, Bali Gham, Bali Gasho and Bali Gangsin followed the Southern Cameroons to the Cameroun Republic.

The coming of independence was particularly animated in Bali Nyonga because many of its elites were actively engaged in the nationalist movement.

Bali Nyonga in Politics

The constituent diversity of Galega's fondom meant that it was a natural hotbed of party politics. It had always been a testing ground for new ideas and projects. The ruling Kamerun National Congress party [KNC] had a vibrant branch in Bali, animated by the fiery Lawrence Ngalam. Galega himself was one of its leading proponents, in which capacity he represented traditional rulers at the Lancaster House Conference of 1957 on the future of the Southern Cameroons.

That Conference was a turning point in the history of the Southern Cameroons, as much for what was accomplished there as for what transpired within the KNC delegation. While in London, Galega II had a massive fall-out with the party leader and Premier, Dr. E.M.L. Endeley, supposedly over his cavalier attitude towards traditional authority. And upon his return home, Galega crossed over to the rival Kamerun National Democratic Party [KNDP] and convinced most of his peers in Bamenda to do the same. Not that the KNDP was new in Bali Nyonga: it had been formed in March 1955 by a group of school masters led by J.N. Foncha from Bafreng and including W.P. Lebaga from Bali.

Galega's departure from the KNC took the wind out of Endeley's sails. At the election of 1959, he lost the premiership of the Southern Cameroons to Foncha, and in the plebiscite of 1961 to determine the future of the Territory, his option to join Nigeria was handsomely defeated by Foncha's option to unite with the Cameroun Republic.

In the early days of unification, Bali Nyonga had a significant presence in the State of West Cameroon. In the domain of representation, Galega was Vice President of the House of Chiefs, while W.S. Fonyonga sat in the House of Assembly, paving the way for eight more parliamentarians from Bali Nyonga.[1] In the central administration, natives of Bali successfully positioned themselves: W.P. Lebaga, J.T. Nchamukong, Michael Sabum, Jomia Pefok and Robert Fortingo soon became household names in Buea, handling strategic positions in the State administration.[2] And in 1966, when all the political parties in the country were merged into the Cameroon National Union, Galega II was unanimously elected to head the new party in Bamenda. Meanwhile, Bali Nyonga developed from a Native Authority to a District, with a resident administration and a local council, and on to a

---

1   Successive Parliamentarians from Bali Nyonga included A.W. Daiga, D.B. Tatah, Cletus Tita, S.P.D. Tita, G.B. Sikod, Ganyonga III, Regina Mundi and Vanigansen Mochiggle.
2   Lebaga was Chairman of the Development Agency, Nchamukong was Secretary to the Prime Minister, Sabum was Clerk of the House of Assembly, Pefok was Secretary to the Public Service Commission, and Fortingo was Second-in-Command of the State Police Force.

Sub-Division, with its own D.O.

But if things looked fairly rosy otherwise for Bali Nyonga, its nemesis in the form of land disputes was always lurking around the corner.

Resurgent Land Problems

After the dramatic events of March 1952, the people of Bali Nyonga yearned for the end of the recurrent land problems with their neighbours. They were comforted by the decision of the Manson Commission of Inquiry that there were no grounds, either legal or equitable, to justify any readjustment of the boundaries between Bali and its neighbours.[3] Justice Manson regarded the security of tenure as a prerequisite for orderly and progressive development, noting that: "There can be no feeling of stability or security if boundaries are continually to be varied or sought to be varied."[4] And for the next decade or so, there was relative calm in the Bali Nyonga neighbourhood.

But following the independence of the Southern Cameroons and its unification with the Cameroun Republic, many thought that the 1953 judgment, which had been delivered in Nigeria, had lapsed. And taking full advantage of the new situation, the Widikum leadership opened fresh disputes with Bali. From every vantage point, subtle hints were made, and open petitions introduced to build grim new stories about Bali Nyonga. The concordant narratives were that the Bali had grabbed so much land for themselves that all their neighbours were virtually squeezed out of existence!

The remonstrations finally induced the Cameroon government to act. In 1977, President Ahidjo issued a Decree modifying the territorial boundaries of the Bali Nyonga fondom and distributing portions of its land to practically all of its neighbours.[5] The decree looked viciously lopsided, taking so much from Bali and giving them nothing in return. But on closer examination, the document itself was something of a lame duck, intentionally or accidentally hamstrung by its central

3 Manson Report, para. 8, cf. *Nigeria Gazette* no. 37, vol. 40, Lagos, 8th June 1953.
4 Ibid.
5 *Decree No. 77-525* Modifying the Territorial Boundaries of certain Traditional Communities in the Mezam and Momo Divisions, Yaounde, 23 Dec. 1977.

operative clause. The 1977 Decree stipulated in essence that natives of Bali Nyonga found in the zones affected by the boundary modifications "may remain where they are, on condition that they submit themselves to the authority of the new traditional ruler having jurisdiction over the area in which they reside."[6] For a people who had braced themselves for the worst, that condition was a welcome bargain. They all opted to stay, meaning that although the boundaries of the fondom had been modified, Bali ownership of the land at stake remained securely intact. In other words, the land was taken from the fondom, but not from the natives. And suddenly, neighbouring Meta chiefs were saddled with land-owning natives of Bali as their new "subjects", knowing fully well that the cultural allegiance of the "newcomers" lay elsewhere. The irony of the Decree was that it technically enabled natives of Bali to own vast expanses of land in the surrounding Meta villages, a dreaded situation that converted the Decree itself into something of a poisoned gift to the Meta people.

Their excitement over the new arrangements lasted only until they realised that the Decree had instead left them in a fix. Their leaders had lobbied for portions of Bali land without any population. Ahidjo gave them groups of reluctant Bali people without any land, since the Decree maintained effective ownership of the land in question with its current occupants. Embarrassed by that unexpected outcome, Meta natives in high places connived with the military to harrass Bali people out of the land, in total violation of the Decree itself.

Tensions flared and confrontation loomed, prompting Ahidjo to dispatch his Minister of Territorial Administration, Victor Ayissi Mvodo, to explain the tenets of the disputed Decree and restore calm.

The encounter of February 1978 was tumultuous. The Bali Community Hall came down when the Minister disingeniously thanked the people for magnanimously "offering" the demarcated land to their estranged neighbours.[7] Galega responded by affirming his position on the matter, that the government was free to allocate any land it wished

---

6   Ibid., Article 8(1).
7   Victor Ayissi Mvodo, *Speech at the Bali Community Hall*, 27 Feb. 1978.

to whoever it chose, but it could not be said that the Bali had offered their land to anybody, because they would never do such a thing.[8] On that principle Galega II had based his reign; on it the people of Bali Nyonga have always stood. The meeting ended in total confusion, and the Decree of 1977 slipped into a stalemate that outlived Galega himself.

On 18 September 1985, a lingering illness finally got the better of the ageing Fon, ending his forty-five-year reign, and closing a remarkable chapter in the history of Bali Nyonga. His passing was like the fall of a mighty baobab, leaving a gaping hole in the traditional forest of the Bamenda grassfields. And he was fittingly mourned, not only by his orphaned kinsmen but by sympathisers from around the country and even beyond. For several months, tribute poured into Bali. The Government hailed his "outstanding contribution to the development of the nation."[9] Solomon Tandeng Muna, the Meta icon of the day, saluted his "dynamic contribution to the struggle for the independence of Cameroon."[10] From abroad, Professor Elizabeth Chilver of Oxford glowingly eulogised him:

> The peaceful transition to independence owes a great deal to his tact, powers of persuasion and personal integrity. He was a very generous-hearted ruler, often in the face of severe obstruction and provocation, and he never allowed personal considerations to obscure his vision of the future.[11]

As a ruler, Galega II always worried about the future, often contemplating the transition towards it. And as he aged, he yearned for stability in the kingdom. He took steps to ensure that when it came, his succession should not be as disputed as his accession had been. And for the first time in Bali history, the throne changed hands without incident.

8   V.S. Galega II, *Speech at the Bali Community Hall*, 27 Feb. 1978.
9   *Speech by the Senior Divisional Officer for Mezam at the Funeral of V.S. Galega II,* Bali, 27 September 1985.
10 S.T. Muna, *Telegramme to the Bali Traditional Council,* 25 September 1985.
11 E.M. Chilver, *Letter to the author,* 14 October 1985.

On 29 September 1985, when the ceremonial buffalo skins shielding the heir were finally lowered, the jammed plaza gasped. Galega had reigned for so long that most in attendance were witnessing the succession ritual for the first time. And they hardly knew the new Fon who emerged from the buffalo skins. Bikai Dohsang, as he was called as a prince, had spent most of his life away from the village, being groomed for that day. From the onset, he showed a keen sense of history: in selecting the regnal name of Ganyonga III, he significantly returned the Fonyonga line of Bali kings to its Mubako roots. And as he wished in his inaugural address for peace and prosperity to all men, many agreed that the torch had effectively been passed to a new generation.

But the harsh realities of the old era cast a grim shadow on that new generation. A few years before Ganyonga's accession, the Fon of Guzang presided over the Lela festival in Bali in the absence of Galega II, meanwhile, trenches were being dug elsewhere to physically separate Bali Nyonga from Mungen Mbu. The hot and cold facets of Bali-Meta relations, which had consumed the essence of Galega's reign, could not be more starkly contrasted.

That curious trench-digging exercise revived the dreaded ghost of the Widikum crisis of 1952, which soon came visiting again, in the form of the Chomba border skirmishes of May 2005 that claimed several lives.

However, the greatest threat to the peace under Ganyonga III came, not from the Widikum, but from within Bali Nyonga itself. A smouldering crisis with Bawock had been brewing for some time. The misunderstanding arose when revisionist elements in Bawock began to claim ownership of the sacred shrine where the Bali cleansed their ritual flags since settlement in 1864. It was an outlandish claim: the Bawock, a Bamileke community from around Bandiangseu near Bangante, had come to Bali in 1906, half a century later, as guests of the TiMbundam, who themselves had been received by Fonyonga II two years earlier. When the latter were removed from Bali in 1911, following a bitter dispute with Fonyonga, he gave their vacated land to the Bawock who camped nearby and had remained loyal to him during the dispute. They lived peacefully, mingling freely with their hosts, until radicals began to sow distrust between the two communities. Things boiled over in 2007, when, for the first time in history, agitators intercepted the "Vòma" cult and desecrated its instruments. The transgression was monstrous because the "Voma" cult was one of the most sacred institutions in the land, held in mystic awe throughout the fondom. It was not seen by the uninitiated in Bali itself. And for it to be publicly profaned in Bawock was a tremendous outrage. A handful of incensed Bali youth descended on Bawock in search of the culprits. What followed was as dramatic as it was controversial. The Bawock claimed that about a hundred houses were burnt in their village on that day, leading to an exodus of all the people to seek government protection in Bamenda. But, on closer examination, no one was killed or injured on either side, neither was a single assailant apprehended. Which raises questions on the fact and nature of the engagement: Who actually burnt the houses? Where were the people when their houses were burning? What did they do, other than seek government protection? Was it possible for the entire village, including children, the elderly, the sick and the disabled, to promptly congregate somewhere, far from home, without intent or organisation? Could it be that upon realising the enormity of the offence and fearing for the worst, the Bawock themselves inflicted symbolic damage on their property to attract government sympathy? Or had the "Voma" incident let off a premeditated plot to vilify their hosts before the court of public opinion by dramatising the day's mock violence? Whatever the case, official reaction quickly went from consternation to indifference as the facts of the incident emerged. In the end, after spending weeks in a make-shift refugee centre in Bamenda, the people of Bawock took advice and returned home, with a few sheets of zinc as token government support for their troubles. It looked like 1952 all over again, when innocent villagers were deceived by unscrupulous agitators to engage in a foredoomed speculative gamble, for which they incurred heavy losses.

The misunderstanding did not distract Bali Nyonga from its search for harmony, within the fondom and in the wider neighbourhood. Although harder times had been known before, the present time was one of excitement and expectation: an ambitious new Fon had been

BALI NYONGA SINCE INDEPENDENCE

enthroned; a modernised stretch of the Trans-African Highway traversed the land, easing travel and facilitating contact; sophisticated structures were sprouting everywhere, constantly changing the landscape of the fondom; in 2004, another landmark was celebrated when Ganyonga III laid the foundation stone of the Cameroon Christian University, not far from where Galega II had planted the Basel Mission College in 1949. A beautiful new homeland was coming to life in Bali Nyonga. The future beckoned.

APPENDIX I

REPORT OF THE COMMISSION OF INQUIRY INTO THE 1952 RIOTS

(Nigeria Gazette, No 45, vol. 39, Lagos, 26 August, 1952)

Your Excellency,

On the 12th of April 1952, you directed that we should hold an inquiry under the provisions of section 3 (b) and (e) of the Collective Punishment Ordinance.

1. The purpose of the inquiry was to investigate the circumstances in which serious disturbances among the Widekum and Bali people lately occurred in the neighbourhood of Bali in the Bamenda Province of the Cameroons; and to ascertain whether all or any inhabitants of any village or district or members of any tribe or community in the neighbourhood of Bali have suppressed or combined to suppress evidence in any criminal case, investigation, inquiry or inquest and whether they have been guilty of such conduct as to require the bringing of soldiers or police to the village or district or the employment of soldiers or police against them for the purposes of preventing or suppressing disturbances or of enforcing lawful orders.

2. We opened our inquiry at the New Hospital, Bamenda, on the 21st April and heard evidence there on the 21st, 22nd, 25th and 26th April. On the 24th April we visited part of the area affected by the disturbances and inspected damage to houses and crops.

3. On the 27th April we proceeded to Bali and sat in the Bali Native Court on the 28th and 29th. On the 1st and 2nd May we heard evidence in the Moghamo Native Court at Batibo. On the 3rd May, we returned to Bamenda.

4. On the 5th May we sat in the Ngemba Native Court, on the 6th in the Resident's Office at Bamenda, and on the 7th in the South

West Federation Native Authority Council Hall at Mbengwi in the Menemo clan area.

5. We conducted our proceedings at Bamenda, Batibo, Mbengwi and Ngemba in public. At the commencement of each sitting we explained the scope of our inquiry to the considerable number of the members of the public who were present. Evidence was taken on oath and recorded. No counsel appeared.

6. We have read Hunt's Report on the Bali People (1925), Newton's Ngemba Intelligence and Re-Assessment Report (1935), Croasdale's Moghamo Intelligence Report (1932) and Menemo Intelligence Report (1933), and Goodliffe's Report on the Reorganisation of the Bali People (1949).

7. The following documents accompany the report:

    a.) The original transcript of the evidence contained in two books which were used alternately and two certified true copies thereof.

    b.) Your Excellency's directions touching the conduct of this inquiry.

    c.) A copy of letter addressed to the Local Councils and Courts of Ngemba, Moghamo, Menemo and Bali and marked Exhibit n° 1.

    d.) Schedule of searches for arms by police produced by Mr E. S. Morgan, Senior Superintendent of Police, and marked Exhibit n° 2.

    e.) Map of area marked Exhibit n° 3.

    f.) Bamenda Native Administration Dispensary Receipt n° 31976 produced by 29th witness and marked Exhibit n° 4.

    g.) Lists of villages and taxable population in Ngemba, Menemo and Moghamo area produced by 1st witness and marked Exhibits n°s 5, 6 and 7 respectively.

    h.) Schedule showing average income of adult taxable males of Ngemba, Menemo and Moghamo clans produced by 1st witness and marked Exhibit n° 8.

8. We heard altogether forty-one witnesses. Of these fourteen were Government officials; eleven were persons whose names were

suggested by the Fon of Bali; and sixteen were members of the Ngemba, Menemo and Moghamo clans. We found it necessary to examine this large number of witnesses partly because the disturbances were so prolonged and spread over so wide an area; and partly because we considered it essential to have witnesses from each of the three Widekum clans concerned. We sat to hear the evidence of the latter in the Native Court or Council Hall of each of the clans at their own request.

9. The Bali people (to whom we shall hereafter refer as the Balis), are subject to a Native Authority consisting of the Fon (or Chief) of Bali in Council and occupy an area of land in the Bamenda Division entirely surrounded by the lands of the Ngemba, Menemo and Moghamo clans of the Widekum tribe. The boundaries of this enclave have been demarcated as the result of a series of actions in Native Courts, of decisions given under the Inter-Tribal Boundaries Settlement Ordinance and by administrative action. The relative position of these is shown approximately on the map attached to this report (Exhibit n° 3). Each of the Moghamo, Menemo and Ngemba clans has a clan council, and all are subject to the South West Federation Native Authority of the Bamenda Division. The Bali Native Authority is not a member of the Federation.

10. The reports which we have studied suggest that the Balis acquired their land in the latter half of the last century by conquest from already established tribes, including the Widekums, and that under German rule they were in a position of paramountcy, which the early British administration sought forcibly but unsuccessfully to maintain. But in 1925 the last of the Widekum villages were allowed to break away from the hegemony of Bali. Since then there has been a long history of hostility, jealousy and litigation between the Balis and the Widekums. They have for several years had a dispute over an area of land which was the basis of two actions in the Supreme Court in which the plaintiffs were Widekums and the defendant the Fon of Bali. These actions were heard at Bamenda on the 25th February last when the plaintiffs were non-suited and ordered to pay costs. On the following day the 1st witness,

the Senior District Officer, Bamenda, was called upon to disperse a mob of about thirty Widekum women who would not let the Judge leave his lodgings. On the 27th February the Senior District Officer, addressed a letter to the Ngemba, Menemo, Moghamo and Bali Local Councils and Courts warning them of the seriousness of any breach of the peace. The Senior District Officer produced a copy of the letter which is attached to our report and marked Exhibit n° 1. On the 2nd March the Senior District Officer sent detachments of police to points where he anticipated trouble; there were however only thirty or forty police stationed at Bamenda under the command of a sergeant-major.

11. On the 3rd March the 1st witness visited the Bali area and found houses burning and men armed with guns, spears and machetes, looting houses: these men were distinguished by the fact that each had a strand of raffia tied round his neck. The witness arrested two of these men with the help of his interpreter, the 4th witness, who identified them by their speech as men of the Moghamo clan. The 1st witness saw parties of armed Balis moving towards the burning houses but persuaded them not to fight; he also stated that he had previously requested the Fon of Bali to restrain his people from any breach of the peace in the event of trespass by the Widekums. After finding a bridge on the Bamenda-Mamfe road in the Moghamo area partially destroyed by fire and still burning, the 1st witness returned to Bamenda and asked the 6th witness, the Resident, Bamenda Province, to telegraph for police reinforcements.

12. On the 4th March in the early morning the 1st witness went to visit a bridge on the Bamenda-Mamfe road in the Ngemba area. On the way a member of the party accompanying him was wounded by a gunshot fired by a person unknown. The 1st witness found that the decking of the bridge had been removed and that a Veterinary Department kit car was lying with its back wheels in the stream. The kit car was on fire and there was a heap of grass burning under its bonnet. The burning and looting continued in the Bali area. An attempt by the 1st witness later in the day to persuade a band of armed men in the Menemo area to return peacefully to

their houses failed and the men advanced into the Bali area. The 4th witness stated that a band of twenty looters whom he saw on the 4th spoke Moghamo.

13. On the 5th March, the 2nd witness, Mr E.S. Morgan, Senior Superintendent of Police, reached Bali with forty-five police from Buea. He ordered his force to split up into detachments and advance towards the burning houses. He and Mr Grey accompanied one detachment. Bands of armed men advanced in extended order as if for battle but on the approach of the police would move slowly back. On at least two occasions when the 2nd witness attempted to approach armed men, he was met by levelled guns. The police at this stage were unable to restore order because they were too few in number. Later in the day two further police units arrived, each of fifty men under an Assistant Superintendent. During the course of the disturbances three other units of the same strength arrived. The 2nd witness stated that he considered the scale of reinforcements no more than necessary to put an end to the disturbances and to prevent a recurrence. We would draw attention to the fact that not a single shot was fired by the police during the disturbances.

14. The police began to get the situation in hand on the 7th but sporadic outbreaks of burning and lootings of Bali houses by bands of armed men continued up to the 14th. The Balis were ordered by the 2nd witness not to take reprisals or go to the perimeter of their land where most of the burning took place and for the most part retired to Bali town in the centre of their area.

15. On the 17th March a company of the 5th Battalion, the Nigeria Regiment, reached Bamenda. The 6th witness, the Resident, Bamenda Province, stated that their presence was undoubtedly instrumental in preventing a recurrence of the disturbances.

16. As a result of the disturbances two men died in Bamenda Hospital and four were brought in dead; of these, four have been identified as Balis, the tribe of the other two has not been established. One Widekum man from Bande in the Ngemba area is known to have been killed. The Balis (14th witness) claimed four killed and one missing; two were identified to the 8th witness at Bamenda

Hospital. The Moghamo clan (38th witness) claimed four missing; none was identified at Bamenda Hospital.

17. The 7th, 10th, 11th, 12th and 13th witnesses, who on the Resident's instructions assessed the damage, found approximately 1,650 dwelling houses and 390 store houses destroyed or seriously damaged by fire; these figures include 130 houses and twenty store houses believed to have belonged to persons of Widekum extraction living on Bali land in the mixed Bali-Widekum settlements of Mengen Muwa, Mengen Mbo and Babossa. All these houses were thatched; and the great majority were constructed of mud and Bamboo. These houses, as we ourselves saw, collapsed completely when burned and were reduced to heaps of charred rubble. Little thatching or building will be possible until the rains are over. The 7th witness estimated the cost of building a mud and bamboo house to be £5-£7, and in the case of a store house, £1.10s-£2. These figures were the lowest given us and we see no reason to disagree with them. Therefore, at a conservative estimate the damage to houses amounts to over £8,000. To this must be added the damage to crops and economic trees described by the witness mentioned above.

We have not found it possible to value this damage, but we are of the opinion that it would amount to a substantial sum. These witnesses were of course unable in every case to make a detailed assessment.

18. Evidence relating to the identity of the armed men who burned and looted Bali houses between the 3rd and 14th March was given by witnesses N°S 14-20 and 22-24, all Balis who claimed to have been present during the disturbances. Although we were on our guard against a natural desire on the part of the Balis to overstate their case, we were impressed by the straightforward and restrained attitude of these witnesses. They identified, generally to our satisfaction, attackers from villages all over the Moghamo and Menemo areas and from the villages in the Ngemba area which lie close to the Bali boundary. Their evidence is to a large extent corroborated by the evidence of the 1st, 3rd, 4th, 5th and 10th witnesses.

19. We also draw attention to the evidence of the 36th witness, Mr McCaffrey, Assistant Superintendent of Police, who stated that out of a total of fifty-six persons convicted up to the 6th May of offences directly connected with the disturbances, fifty-two came from the Moghamo, Menemo and Ngemba clan areas; the remaining four came from the mixed settlements of Mengen Muwa and Mengen Mbo and were persons of Widekum sympathies.

20. The witnesses from the Moghamo, Menemo and Ngemba clans appeared for the most part to be chiefly interested in establishing their personal innocence, although at the commencement of our sessions, at Batibo and Ngemba Native Courts and at Mbengwi, we were at pains to explain the purpose of our inquiry. The 33rd witness, I No Lie Ndanin, however, at Batibo stated that the Balis attacked the Widekums in the mixed Bali-Widekum settlement of Mengen Muwa which is on Bali land. He said that Widekums from outside Mengen Muwa came to their fellow clansmen's assistance and that they came unarmed. In spite of the witness's name, he did not impress us as a truthful witness; his answers to questions were evasive and his manner extremely uneasy. We consider it impossible to place any reliance on his evidence. We note that the 12th witness, Mr Wood, District Officer stated that out of a total of 292 houses burned in Mengen Muwa 219 had apparently been the property of Balis. We note also that widespread attacks on Bali houses all over the Bali area took place on the same day as houses were burned in Mengen Muwa.

21. When we sat in the Ngemba Native Court on the 5th May the Ngemba clansmen present were emphatic that only Ndefru, the President of their Council, could speak for them. It was necessary to send for Ndefru and, while he waited, we ourselves called the 34th witness, a village head of the Ngemba area. When Ndefru, (35th witness), arrived his evidence was almost entirely directed towards establishing the fact that he was in hospital during the disturbances; he did however state under cross-examination that his people fought the Balis because they heard a drum in Mengen Muwa but was unwilling to develop the theme. We note from Exhibit n° 3 that Bande, Ndefru's village, is about twelve miles from

Mengen Muwa in a direct line. The 34th witness also said that the Ngembas fought the Balis but made no excuse for them and did not refer to Mengen Muwa. Before leaving Ngemba Native Court on the 5th we announced our intention of sitting at Bamenda on the following day. No Ngembas appeared on the 6th.

22. At Mbengwi on the 7th May the 37th witness, the village head of a Widekum section of the mixed Bali-Widekum village of Mengen Mbo, claimed that the Balis attacked his people in Mengen Mbo, burned their houses and turned them out. He said that he did not know who burned 236 houses in Mengen Mbo which the 13th witness, Mr Elkerton, had stated to be the property of the Balis; and that he had no knowledge of any Bali houses being burned anywhere. We received the impression that this witness's evidence in chief had been rehearsed; it broke down under cross-examination. We would apply the same remarks to the 39th witness. We cannot accept their evidence.

23. The two Presidents of the Moghamo and Ngemba Clan Councils, the 28th and 35th witnesses respectively, each sought to establish that he was away during the disturbances and was in no way responsible for what occurred. The 28th witness admitted receiving Exhibit n° 1 before leaving his village for Mamfe. Apart from the 28th and 35th witnesses no less than four Widekum village heads of the six who gave evidence endeavoured to establish alibis and their example was also followed by a Widekum Native Court member (32nd witness). We find it difficult to believe that the similarity of so many claims is a mere coincidence.

24. We found on the other hand the evidence of the President of the Menemo Clan Council (41st witness) most illuminating. This witness was nervous as might well be expected in the presence of some 150 or so of his clansmen whose attitude was truculent and hostile. But we gained the impression that he spoke the truth and wished to be of assistance.

25. We note that a small proportion of Widekum houses in Mengen Muwa and Mengen Mbo was burned. We carefully tested the allegations that it was the Balis who burned these houses in an unprovoked attack on the Widekums. Not only were we not

impressed by the demeanour of the witness who made these allegations, but we consider their contention intrinsically unlikely in the light of the evidence (which we accept) of widespread attacks on Bali settlements at a great many other points on the perimeter of their land on the morning of the 3rd March. From considerations of time and distance we think it most unlikely that appeals for help from Mengen Muwa and Mengen Mbo could have been answered so quickly by attacks on so many other Bali settlements. While we cannot exclude the possibility of retaliation by the Balis, we think it likely that the Widekum houses which were destroyed in the mixed settlements were burned in the general conflagration.

26. The widespread area over which the disturbances took place and the extent of the damage lead us to believe that a very large number of persons took part and that a considerable proportion of the inhabitants of the areas adjacent to Bali lands must be fully aware of what occurred. But neither in this inquiry nor in the inquiries carried out by the Administration and the Nigeria Police have the people of the Moghamo, Menemo and Ngemba clans shown any willingness to co-operate or assist. The attitude of the Presidents of the Moghamo and Ngemba Clan Councils has already been described. The evidence of the 3rd and 7th witness, Mr McCaffery, states that the Widekum clansmen have given the police virtually no assistance, although the Balis have been helpful throughout.

27. We accept the evidence of the 6th witness, the Resident of Bamenda Province, that certain villages in the Ngemba clan area were not concerned in the disturbance; i.e., Bapinyi, Bambullue, Bagangu (otherwise known as Akum), Banjong, Bafawkum, Bafawmissang, Santa, Abakpa (a stranger settlement), and Bamenda Government Station. We note that these villages are situated at a distance from the Bali boundary and such evidence concerning them as we have heard is slight.

28. On the 9th May when this report had for the most part been completed and typed, we received from a Mr E.F. Fawty a written address which we attach hereto. We have considered its contents and observe that in so far as it repeats the allegations that the Balis made an unprovoked attack on the Widekums, we have

already dealt with this contention in paragraphs 20 and 22; the remainder is outside our terms of reference. We would add that Mr Fawty was given the opportunity of giving evidence on oath but declined to do so.

Conclusions

29. To summarise our conclusions with respect to the points into which Your Excellency directed us to inquire:

1) In our opinion the responsibility for the disturbances lies with the Moghamo, Menemo and Ngemba clans of the Widikum tribe, subject to the exceptions set out in paragraph 27.

2) The attacks on Bali property were planned and concerted; they were carried out by a large number of persons over a period of more than one week. A considerable proportion of the Moghamo, Menemo and Ngemba clans must be fully aware of what occurred. These people however, including their village heads and two clan council presidents, have given little or no information or assistance in the inquiries which have been made. We consider that their conduct amounts to a combined effort to suppress evidence.

3) The conduct of the Moghamo, Menemo and Ngemba clans has been such as to require the bringing of police and soldiers to the districts in which they live and the employment of police against them for the purpose of suppressing disturbances and preventing a recurrence of such disturbances.

Recommendations

30. We recommend that Your Excellency should impose a fine under the provisions of section 3 of the Collective Punishment Ordinance upon all the indigenous inhabitants of the Moghamo group area, the Menemo clan area and the Ngemba clan area of the Bamenda Province as indicated in Public Notice N° 116 of 1949; except that we recommend that the inhabitants of the following villages in the Ngemba clan area should be exempted from such fine: Bapinyi, Bambullue, Bagangu, Banjong, Bafawkum, Bafawmissang, Santa, Abakpa and Bamenda Government Station.

31. We recommend that the amount of the fine should be ten thousand pounds. In arriving at this figure, we have borne in mind that any fine imposed should be large enough to constitute an appropriate punishment to those concerned in the disturbances, to serve as a deterrent and a warning against recurrences, and to afford to the Balis a measure of compensation commensurate, in so far as possible, with their losses. We have on the other hand given careful consideration to the question of what amount those concerned may reasonably be called upon to pay. To this end we have examined figures showing the tax rates, the taxable population and the estimated average income of adult males in the areas concerned.

32. We have not taken into consideration any sum which those concerned may be ordered to pay under the provisions of section 11 of the Peace Preservation Ordinance. We respectfully recommend that any fine which Your Excellency may see fit to order to be paid as a result of this report should be taken into account if any sum becomes payable under the provisions of that Ordinance.

33. We recommend that of the total fine nine thousand pounds shall be applied in compensation to the Balis and other indigenous inhabitants of the Bali Native Authority area for the injuries caused to them as a result of the disturbances; and that this sum should be administered at the discretion of the Resident, Bamenda Province.

34. We recommend further that any date which may be ordered by Your Excellency for the payment of a fine imposed as a result of this report shall be not less than three months after the date of such order.

35. Although not within our terms of reference, we feel it our duty respectfully to suggest that, in view of the tension which still exists between the Balis and the Widekums, a substantial police force be retained in the Bamenda Province at least until any fine imposed under this Ordinance has been collected.

(Signed) E. C. ALDERTON
(Signed) D. L. BATE
(Signed) ABDUL AZIZ ATTA

Dated at Bamenda this 12th day of May, 1952.

Note: *The documents referred to in paragraphs 7 and 28 above have not been printed.*

APPENDIX II

Nigeria Order made under the Collective Punishment Ordinance N° 33 of 1952 (Cap. 34)

Whereas on the twelfth day of April, 1952, it was directed that an inquiry be held for the purposes of the Collective Punishment Ordinance to inquire into the circumstances in which disturbances of the Queen's peace involving the Widekum and Bali peoples had occurred in the neighbourhood of Bali in the Bamenda Province of the Cameroons, in order to ascertain whether all or any inhabitants of any village or district or members of any tribe or community in the neighbourhood aforesaid had,

    a.) suppressed, or combined to suppress, evidence in any criminal case, investigation or inquiry, or in any inquest, or

    b.) been guilty of such conduct as to require the bringing of soldiers or police to the village or district or the employment of soldiers or police against them for the purposes of preventing or suppressing disturbances of the character aforesaid or enforcing lawful orders;

And whereas the inquiry has been duly held.

And whereas the Governor, upon consideration of the evidence taken at the said inquiry and the report upon that evidence made by the officers who conducted the said inquiry, finds that the members of the Moghamo, Menemo and Ngemba clans of the Widikum tribe, with the exception of the inhabitants of Bapinyi, Bambullue, Bagangu, Banjong, Bafawkum, Bafawmissang, Santa and Abakpa villages, and Bamenda Government Station, combined to suppress evidence in investigations and inquiries relating to the said disturbances, and further that the conduct of the members of the communities afore-said has been such as to require the bringing of soldiers and police to the districts in which they live and the employment of police against members of the said communities for the purpose of preventing and suppressing disturbances;

Now, therefore, in exercise of the powers conferred upon the Governor by section 3 of the Collective Punishment Ordinance, the following Order is hereby made:

1. This Order may be cited as the Collective Punishment (Widekum) Order, 1952.
2. It is hereby ordered that:

   a.) a fine of ten thousand pounds be imposed on all the indigenous inhabitants of the Moghamo group area, the Menemo clan area and the Ngemba court area (as indicated in Public Notice n° 116 of 1949) with the exception of the inhabitants of the following villages, that is to say, Bapinyi, Bambullue, Bagangu (otherwise known as Akum), Banjong, Bafawkum, Bafawmissang, Santa and Abapka villages, and Bamenda Government Station; and

   b.) of the said fine the sum of nine thousand pounds be applied in such manner as the Resident, Bamenda Province, shall think fit in compensation to the Balis and other indigenous inhabitants of the Bali Native Authority area for the injuries caused to them by the disturbances to which the aforesaid investigations and inquiries related; and

   c.) that the said fine shall be paid on or before the twenty-fifth day of September, 1952.

Made at Lagos this 26th day of August, 1952.
By His Excellency's Command,

L. H. GOBLE,
Acting Chief Secretary to the Government.

APPENDIX III

THE MANSON REPORT

(Nigeria Gazette, n° 37, vol. 40, Lagos, 8th June 1953)

Your Excellency,

1. I was appointed by Your Excellency under the Commissions of Inquiry Ordinance (Chapter 37) to be sole Commissioner of Inquiry into certain land disputes between the Widikum and the Bali peoples in the Bamenda Division of the Cameroon under United Kingdom Trusteeship. The precise terms of reference of the Commission will be found at pages 1, 2. I held twenty-three Meetings. The proceedings were unduly protracted owing to double interpretations as each party desired to have its own special interpreter. In some cases, the interpretation was treble when an interpreter in a special dialect had to be employed.

2. I feel that I should explain very shortly the circumstances which occasioned this Inquiry. From time to time over a period of years between twenty-five and thirty years -- there have been disputes over land between the Bali people — or more precisely the Bali Nyonga Branch of the Bali people — and some of their Widikum neighbours. These disputes resulted in many petitions and from time to time in boundary demarcations by Administrative Officers, by agreement between the parties or under the Inter-Tribal Boundaries Settlement Ordinance (Chapter 95). Eventually in 1948-49 Mr F. A. Goodliffe, Senior District officer was appointed to hold an Inquiry under the Ordinance with a view to determining a boundary which was in dispute between the Bali people and a Widikum community — the Bamengen (Mengen Mbo). The land which was the subject matter of M. Goodliffe's Inquiry is part of the land in dispute in those suits referred to in the terms of reference

of this present Inquiry. Mr Goodliffe's Inquiry resulted in a finding of fact that the Mengen Mbo people had lost all their rights over the land in dispute to the Bali people who had acquired the land from them by conquest sometime before 1890 and therefore, it was not possible to fix a boundary between them. The material parts of M. Goodliffe's report will be found in Appendix B. I have extracted them because the nature of the claim in this case in respect of the area verged yellow in Plan A in folder and much repetition will be avoided. The representatives of the Mengen Mbo community applied to the Chief Commissioner under section 7 of the Ordinance for a review of M. Goodliffe's decision. The Chief Commissioner confirmed M. Goodliffe's finding and stated that there were no merits in the appeal. At the same time the representative of the Mengen Mbo Community was informed by letter that the Chief Commissioner "was advised that Mr Goodliffe's judgment as confirmed, will not preclude the Mengen people from commencing proceedings in Court for a declaration of title. Should they elect to commence proceedings in Court, the case will be transferred to the Supreme Court where no accusations of prejudice can be levelled at the Judge."

As a result, the Mengen Mbo people instituted an action against the Fon of Bali in the Bali Native Court which was transferred to the Supreme Court by an Order of Transfer under section 28 of the Native Courts Ordinance (chapter 142). Suit N° C/33/1950. The claim, as stated in the Summons, was "ownership of Mengen Mbo land in Bali area taken by the Defendant through the Government or British Administrative Officers since 1922." At the same time eight other Widikum communities surrounding Bali jointly instituted an action against the Fon of Bali claiming a declaration of title of portions of Bali land, damages and injunction against the Defendant, restraining him and his people from entering on the land and interfering with the Plaintiff's use and enjoyment of it -- Suits N° C/55/50, N° 0/64/50 and N° 0/65/50. These suits were also transferred to the Supreme Court and were consolidated with Suit N° 0/33/50. A certified copy of the Summonses and Orders of Transfer will be found in Appendix E.

The course which the proceedings took in the Supreme Court can be seen by referring to a certified copy of the proceedings in Appendix E. It is sufficient to say that the Plaintiffs in the consolidated suits were nonsuited on the ground that they had not pleaded title under the Land and Native Rights Ordinance (Chapter 105, section 4), and that no title could be granted to them except by the Governor and that, without such title, their claim to damages and an injunction could not be entertained. This abrupt rejection of their claims without any evidence being called except that of the surveyor was the immediate occasion of an outbreak of violence by the Widikum people some few days later. One may perhaps, make this passing observation. The Mengen Mbo community were informed directly — and the other Widikum communities indirectly — by the Chief Commissioner whom they regarded as the Governor, that they could, if they so wished, pursue their claim to a declaration of title in the Supreme Court. They acted on this suggestion and were then informed by the Judge that he could not grant the declaration they sought and that they should apply to Governor. Without justifying their conduct, one must, in fairness, say that the Widikum people were very understandably mystified, if not bewildered, at the dilemma in which they found themselves. The Governor told them to go to the Court and the Court told them to go to the Governor. The sudden termination, with heavy costs, of their suits which had involved them in very considerable expenditure on account of lawyer's and surveyor's fees, for reasons which they probably did not understand and without any witness, except the surveyor being called, imposed too heavy a strain on their patience and they took the law into their own hands. There can be little doubt that they were encouraged, if not instigated and indeed organised by their leaders.

3.   The nature of the claim by the Widikum people is simple. The Court in the consolidated suits ordered pleadings to be filed by both parties and a Plan to be filed by the Plaintiffs. In consequence, the nature of the claim and of the defence and the exact area in dispute are precisely defined. The Plan filed by the Plaintiffs will be found in the folder at the end of this Report (Plan A). It was an agreed Plan (see Appendix E). Another Plan on a smaller scale

is also to be found in the folder (Plan B). It is a copy of the Plan which was filed at the Inquiry held by Mr Goodliffe. A copy of the Pleadings will be found in Appendix E. The actual area in dispute is the area verged purple, excluding the central area verged red to which the Widikums lay no claim. The total extent of these two areas is about 130 square miles. In 1948-49 the Bali population was estimated at 12.397. A reference to the Plan A will show an area verged yellow which is approximately the area claimed by the Mengen Mbos, a Widikum community, at M. Goodliffe's Inquiry in 1948-49. The Widikum case can be put very shortly. They assert that the area verged red was given to the Bali people when the latter first arrived in the area about 125 years ago. They say that Bali Nyongas, who are the Defendants, were in flight from another Bali branch called Bali Kumbat and came to them as strangers seeking their protection and they were granted the area verged red called "Wumkai" for settlement and also were assisted by the Widikums to drive back the Bali Kumbats. The alleged gift of land is said to have been accompanied by some ceremony at which a fig tree was planted. They allege that they lived in peace with the Bali Nyongas for many years until the time of the first German arrival which was about 1886. The Widikums say that the Balis sought favour with the Germans and, with German assistance, and later with British co-operation, encroached beyond the confines of the area verged red and occupied the land and acquired suzerainty over the Widikum communities who were settled on the area outside it (see paragraphs 8, 9, 10 of the Statement of Claim: Appendix E). The Widikums lay no claim to the area verged red, which one may call the "gifted" area. The land in dispute is thus all that area of land lying outside and around the "gifted" land called "Wumkai" up to the purple line.

The Bali Nyongas in their defence assert that the Widikum's claim to have given them the present site of Bali Nyonga alias "Wumkai" has no historical foundation. They state that the present site of Bali Nyonga and all the land on all sides up to the purple line were first acquired by conquest from the Widikum indigenous inhabitants by another branch of the Bali people called Bali Kontan and that the Bali Kontans were, in their turn, conquered by the Bali Nyongas about 1830 who then occupied the land and allowed the subject Widikum people to remain and farm on portions of the land, if they so wished, on payment of tribute, paragraph 5 of the Statement of Defence: Appendix E. The Widikum people deny that there ever were any such people as the Bali Kontans, saying that "Kontan" is merely a corruption of the Widikum word "Kwatad" which means "seven" and that the original gift of land had been made to seven Bali Nyonga men who arrived and sought protection of the Widikums when fleeing from Bali Kumbat (see Appendix B). It may be pointed out that Bali Kontans are expressly referred to in Mr Newton's Intelligence Report on Ngemba, Appendix C; see also Bali's seventh witness, page 174.

The Bali Nyongas state that their conquest of the Bali Kontans and their acquisition of the land in dispute by conquest took place fifty or sixty years before the German's first arrival in about 1886 and that the Germans found them to be in full and effective and undisturbed occupation of the area in dispute and that they received no assistance from the Germans or later from the British in acquiring the present site of Bali Nyonga alias "Wumkai" or the surrounding land verged purple (see the evidence of the Bali spokesman).

The above is a summary of the respective claims of the parties.

4. It will be seen from the preceding paragraphs that the issue in the case resolves itself into the questions "Did the Bali Nyongas come to their present site of Bali Nyonga alias "Wumkai", i.e. area verged red as refugees or as conquerors?" and "How did they come to occupy the area outside "Wumkai", i.e. the land bounded by the purple line?

In addition to the evidence recorded by me there has been made available both to the parties themselves and myself many Intelligence Reports compiled by various Administrative Officers covering a period of thirty-six years commencing with the Report of 1916-17 on the Bamenda Division by M. G. S. Podevin, the first British Civil Administrative Officer to be posted to this area after the outbreak of the First World War. These Reports concerning the Balis and the Widikum people (Ngemba, Moghamo, etc.) contain a great deal of historical data. In addition, the parties have had full and free access to many relevant minute papers containing official correspondence and reports of proceedings of Inter-Tribal Boundary Inquiries held by Administrative Officers into disputed land boundaries between the Bali people and their Widikum neighbours, Bambutu, Bametchom, Babad (Baba II), Bafawchu, Pinyin, Asong, Gujang (Moghamo), Esum (Bamenjong), Kai, Nyas, Tunyang, Cobyang, Bande (see Plan A all-round the purple line). These administrative inquiries cover a period of thirty years. In fact, there is so much material available in regard to the Bali people and their relationship with their Widikum neighbours and indeed, with their non-Widikum neighbours, e.g., Bafut, Banso, that there is a danger of not seeing the wood for the trees. I have extracted some material parts of the Report on the Bali Clan prepared by the late Sir William Hunt in 1925 as it is referred to so frequently in the evidence and also in Mr Goodliffe's Inquiry (see Appendix A).

5. I do not propose to analyse or even to summarise the oral and documentary evidence which is material to the issue before this Inquiry. I am not writing a history of the Bali people. It is quite clear to me — the evidence is overwhelming — that the Balis arrived as warriors — well armed for those days, well organised and partially mounted on horses — and subjugated many of the indigenous people whom they found in this area, including many of the Widikum communities. It is agreed that their first arrival was about 1820 or 1825. Dr Zintgraff, the first German explorer who arrived in 1889, was of the opinion that they had arrived about seventy-five years prior to his arrival. This approximate date is, in fact, accepted by the Widikum spokesman. There can be little doubt that the long period of seventy-five years which elapsed between the Bali arrival and the German arrival was occupied in perpetual raiding and counterraiding. It is not, I think, possible at the present day to obtain any additional information as to the

ebb and flow of tribal warfare during this period. There is little possibility now of obtaining fresh data in regard to these local strifes of a hundred years ago or more. Only vague and confused incidents are handed down imperfectly by tradition which tends to become more shadowy as the years go by. One cannot, now, gather from them any connected or coherent story.

It is essential to deal with facts as they are today and as they are known to have been for three-quarters of a century and more. Dr Zintgraff asserts that, on his arrival in 1889, he found the Bali people "the most feared of the inland tribes and their friendship a necessary preliminary to the exploration of the North Cameroons" (paragraph 19 of the Hunt Report). There are no grounds for supposing that this state and reputation of the Bali people of which Dr Zintgraff speaks were of recent origin at that date. Moreover, the Bali people have, since that date, been in actual, effective and, except for an attempt at re-settlement by the Mengen Mbo people in 1921 and 1934, undisturbed occupation of the area in dispute.

In the absence of any reliable, fresh evidence, it is not now possible to reject the version of Bali history contained in the Hunt Report. Its general accuracy in its broad lines must be accepted. Indeed, this Report is the locus classicus and the foundation of the official summary of Bali history to be found in the Report on the Cameroons under the United Kingdom Trusteeship for 1950 and the Report prepared for the Visiting Mission of the Trusteeship Council to the Cameroons under the United Kingdom Trusteeship in 1950; see Appendix C.

The Honourable S.T. Muna is a teacher with educational qualifications and yet he has produced no new historical data to support the Widikum claim or to disprove the general truth of the history as recorded in the Hunt and other Reports and as accepted in the official summary to be found in the Reports to the United Nations. He confined himself to an ineffectual critical analysis, which was not easy to record, of the evidence at Mr Goodliffe's Bali-Bamengen Inter-Tribal Boundary settlement and to an attempt to prove that the Hunt version is based on wrong deductions. The Widikum spokesmen and witnesses persistently deny with wearisome repetition — any conquest and acquisition of their land by the Bali people at any time and refute their alleged vassalage to the Bali people and any suggestion that they were ever at any time under the protection or yoke of the Bali people. They state quite frankly that the Hunt version of history is unreliable as he was misled by corrupt Bali Interpreters (see paragraph 122 of Hunt Report; Appendix A). It is difficult to see how Dr Zintgraff's statement above can be regarded as suspect; he stated what he found. It is not necessary to inquire now how far the Balis carried their conquests or to ascertain the degree of their suzerainty over the Widikum communities whom they attacked. There can be little doubt that the Balis and the Germans were of mutual assistance to one another and that with the German aid the Balis were able to conquer the Bandes, a Widikum community, whom they had been unable to conquer unaided.

It may be that the extent of Bali conquests or suzerainty in 1884 just before the first German arrival as shown in the Map attached to the Hunt Report — a copy of the Plan is in the folder; Plan C -- cannot be regarded as entirely exact and that the Bali claim to the large area of suzerainty granted to them by the Germans in 1905 cannot, historically speaking, be accepted (see final paragraph: Cameroons Report for Visiting Commission of the United Nations in Appendix C). But the point is not of any practical importance at the present day though it may be of some historical interest. No question arises now of vassalage, suzerainty or yokedom — whichever word one may use — of Widikum people by the Balis. The Fon of Bali sets up no such claim now.

The surrounding Widikum communities, whatever may have been the case in the past, are now free and independent peoples; it is not necessary to trace the steps by which their freedom was gained.

There can be no doubt that the Balis acquired the area in dispute and other areas by right of conquest during a period when there was much movement and tribes were migrating and seeking new settlements. The Balis drove the occupants away and formed their own settlement on the land so acquired. The extent to which the Widikum communities were dispossessed of their land no doubt differed; some, e.g., Tunyang, Cobyang, Nya, Kai, were given their land back again as the Balis did not want it. Others, such as Bafawchu, Bametchom were permitted to settle on and farm, in common with the Balis, certain areas of the land which the Balis had acquired from them by conquest and were also given other sites in substitution. Others such as Mbufung, Babossa, Babakus and many Mengens settled with the permission of the Fon of Bali on the conquered land and inter-married with Balis and have become "naturalized" with them and live peaceably amongst them. Eventually, boundaries were demarcated, over a period of many years, between some of the Widikum communities and the Balis, as I have already stated (see also paragraph 8).

No Widikum community has acquired by Bali acquiescence or in any other manner adverse to the Bali people any exclusive rights of occupation over the disputed land or any part of it since the Balis acquired it from them. The Balis have never at any time acknowledged that any Widikum peoples have acquired any rights over the land in dispute or any part of it except those rights of farming and settlement conferred on them by the Fon of Bali as the overlord of the land in dispute.

6. I find myself unable to accept the Widikum version of how the Balis acquired the land now in dispute. The evidence about the "gifted land" i.e. "Wumkai", the area verged red is unconvincing. No definite boundaries were fixed at the time when "Wumkai" was alleged to have been granted to the Bali people; it is said by the 1st Widikum witness to have been demarcated in about 1825, but there is no evidence to show in what manner it was demarcated or by whom or what the boundary marks were. It is also not clear as to which Widikum community granted the land to the Balis. Two witnesses say it was the Mengen Mbos (see 9th Widikum witness and evidence of Fawty at Mr Goodliffe's Inquiry: Appendix B); another witness (2nd Widikum witness) said that it was the Chief of Bande (Mankon) who is said to have been the Paramount Chief of all the Widikum communities at

that date. He was not, in fact, the Paramount Chief at that date. It is doubtful whether he is so now. Another witness (4th Widikum witness) said it was his people the Bambutu and also the Ngemba, Menemo, and Moghamo people.

Then again, there is a conflict of evidence as to what the nature of the gift was. Two Widikum witnesses said that it was free and unconditional (5th and 9th Widikum witness); another witness said that after the gift the Balis remained free and independent (5th Widikum witness). The 2nd Widikum witness said that the Balis in return for this gift were "expected" to catch animals for them and also to assist them to fight Bafut. These acts of servile vassalage are irreconcilable with independence.

Further, I could not discover any adequate reason why the Widikums should have granted this land to the Balis. One witness stated that the "gifted land" was the common Widikum hunting grounds (13th Widikum witness). I cannot believe that such hospitality and such generosity would have been shown in those days to persons who were strangers — and a very considerable number — one witness said 200. Neither do I understand why the Widikums should, as they said they did, have rendered assistance to Bali Nyonga against the other Bali clan viz. Bali Kumbat. The Widikums would appear to have got nothing in return for their assistance. If the Widikums, other than Bande, never, as they say, fought the Bali Nyongas, it can be reasonably inferred as probable that this was because they preferred to submit to a more powerful opponent; alternatively, because they had already been subjugated by the Bali Kontans, the predecessors of the Bali Nyongas (see Bali 7th witness).

The Widikum claim is not only that there was no conquest by Bali, but that the Balis only acquired possession of the area outside the area edged red with German and British aid. As far as German assistance goes, it is quite plain that this area had been acquired, between forty and fifty years before the German arrival, by conquest from the original occupiers by the Bali Kontans who were in turn defeated by the Bali Nyongas. The summons in 0/33/1950 (Appendix E) shows the Widikum (Mengen Mbo) claim against the British Government. The position can be seen in Mr Hunt's Memorandum in Appendix A and the Goodliffe Report paragraphs 5, 6 et seq. Appendix B. It was not a question of what the Widikum spokesman so often calls "the iron hand of Government" depriving them of their land; they were ejected from it because they were attempting to re-occupy land which had been acquired from them by the Balis by conquest many years before. This attempt to return to their original sites was opposed by the Fon of Bali who sought the assistance of the British Administration. The account of the action taken and the reasons for it given by Mr Hunt is so full and so plain that I see no purpose in summarising it. It makes it apparent that there is no foundation for the Widikum allegation that it was the British Government who forcibly deprived them of their land and gave it to the Balis.

7. At the present time, there are some Widikum people living and farming on the land in dispute including the "Wumkai" land. These are the Mbos, Mengen Muwa, Babossa, Mbufung, Babakus, Kunyang, Bamudum. The total number of these probably does not now amount to more than about 250 taxable males. I would refer to paragraph 27 of Mr Goodliffe's Report (Appendix B). His figures — and only approximate figures — were those in 1949. Since then there have been a number of Mengen Mbos and Mengen Muwas who, either during or after the recent disturbances, left the land in dispute for reasons which are not quite apparent and went to neighbouring Widikum communities.

    The Mengen Mbos are not in any defined area; they dwell and farm in Bali Nyonga township and in a few scattered farms on the area in dispute (N. and N.E. of the area verged red). The Mengen Muwas occupy with Bali people a small village at Mile 74 on the Mamfe-Bamenda road (West of the land in dispute). Babossa is N.W. of Plan, Mbufung is S.E. of Mengen Muwa and Bamudum and Babaku are Widikum quarters inside Bali Nyonga township; Kunyang are scattered. It is necessary to refer to these communities because the Widikum people, apart from their claim, as the indigenous occupiers, to the ownership of the land in dispute which, they say, they have never lost by conquest to the Bali people, are putting up, if this claim is rejected, an alternative claim, based on compassionate grounds, to an adjustment of the Bali boundary verged purple. They are making a plea "ad misericordiam." They state that the Mengens and others are not willing to remain and farm on Bali land any longer owing to what the Honourable S.T. Muna has called "the intolerable conditions" under which they live on Bali land, and, therefore, they wish to migrate elsewhere where it would be possible for them to live according to their own laws and customs without interference by the Balis. The Balis do not want any independent unit of the Widikum people to be resident on Bali land and they made an offer to the Widikum spokesmen to withdraw the Bali boundary, i.e. purple line on the Mengen Mbo and Mengen Muwa side in the direction of Bali Nyonga and these two communities would then move from their present site to the other side of the retracted boundary and thus be outside Bali land. The Widikums rejected this offer. Their counteroffer was that the existing settlements should remain where they are and that the boundary line should be so retracted that they would be outside Bali Land. (I would refer to my Note at the end of the 6th Meeting). It is sufficient to say that nothing came of these alternative proposals. A Conciliation Committee consisting of a Neutral Group, a Bali Group and a Widikum Group was set up while the Inquiry was continuing, but, after a considerable number of meetings, it achieved nothing. The Bali offer has now been withdrawn as no agreement was reached. I have not thought it necessary to refer to these abortive deliberations in detail or to include them in this Report. I wish to say, however, that if the alleged "Widikum sufferings" have any real foundation, there is nothing to prevent those who do not wish to remain on Bali land leaving it and joining any other Widikum community outside. I see no reason why the Balis should be expected to give those Widikums who prefer to leave Bali territory any portion of Bali land to settle on; as the Fon of Ngaw put it "would anyone give a shovel to a wife who has decided to leave him and find a new husband?"

I am satisfied that the picture drawn by the Widikum spokes-men and witnesses of the hardships and deprivations and illegal exactions and the other particulars of the "intolerable conditions" is heavily over-drawn and highly coloured and not a truthful representation of the situation. I have no belief in these persons' sincerity. I find that their grievances have no foundation whatever. Their alleged "sufferings" are a figment of their imagination if, indeed, they have not been disingenuously concocted to sup-port their claim. I endeavoured to ascertain the truth about these grievances but was not able to obtain any evidence which I regard as convincing. The Honourable S.T. Muna was vague and uncat-egorical. He himself admits that he has no personal grievances. The Commission was informed that it was intended to call his elder brother, M. Joseph Muna who is the son-in-law of the Fon of Bali, as a witness to substantiate these charges. I was expecting to hear his testimony. He did not appear for reasons which I was unable to ascertain. The Honourable S.T. Muna lived and taught for years in schools in Bali Nyonga. Both these two gentlemen are, therefore, in a position to speak about the sufferings, if any, of their people in Bali Nyonga. One failed to come forward; the other made vague allegations which are not substantiated by other reliable testimony.

There can be little doubt that there are many Widikum people who are living contentedly and peacefully and without any jus-tifiable grounds for complaint in Bali Nyonga township and the outlying farmlands. Babossa are quite contented to remain where they are; and they have been so for the last thirty years (see Note on Babossa in the Hunt Report, Appendix A). They are not a party to these proceedings — in name at any rate — and I am quite satisfied that they seek no redress and make no claim against the Balis. Neither do the Babakus, a handful of Widikums in Bali Nyonga: see 2nd Bali witness — Songwet, page 154; nor do the Mbufung (see page 139); nor have many of the Mengen Mbos in Bali Nyonga (see Bali 4th witness pages 161, 162).

The only representative of Mengen Muwa who spoke about the grievances of Widikums in Mengen Muwa was Jacob Bojia (page 96), whose personal bitterness against the Fon of Bali over the headship of Mengen Muwa village which contains both Widikums and Bali people makes his evidence untrustworthy. He is also shown to have falsely stated that he is the officially recognised Village Head of Mengen Muwa (pages 99, 100). I have said that I reject entirely the allegations of ill-treatment of or discrimination against the Widikum people by the Bali people. There is evidence to show that Widikum people on Bali land are accepted by the Balis as citizens having equal rights. They have inter-married, they attend the same schools at Bali Nyonga, they are permitted to choose their own Quarter or Village Head, and there is no reliable evidence to show that they are not permitted freely to perform their own customs and religious ceremonies without interference by the Balis.

8. I must say something about those Widikum communities who have a common boundary with the Bali people outside the periphery of the land in dispute. Their claims — C/55/1950, 0/64/1950 — pursued in conjunction with the small number of persons belonging to the Widikum Mengen Mbo community inside the periphery, amount to a claim (apart from damages and an injunction) to the whole area of the land in dispute between the red and purple lines. They admit that, if successful in their claim, they will squeeze those Balis living and farming on the area between the red and purple lines back into the area verged red, but will, at the same time, as an acknowledgment of their title, generously consider allowing the Bali people, as compensation, an extension of the area verged red "sufficient to meet their needs." Subject to this, they propose to share amongst themselves the Bali land allotted to them.

    Only two Widikum communities have stated the extent of their claim — the Bafawchus (7th Widikum witness) who claim as far as Benekor (SW. of area verged red) and the Bametchoms W. of Plan (3rd Widikum witness) who claim up to Mile 85 on the Mamfe-Bamenda road. It would be extremely optimistic for anyone to suppose that this distributive share-out of Bali land amongst the various Widikum communities would be effected without considerable disagreements and disputes amongst themselves resulting in litigations and, perhaps, less peaceful forms of settlement. I have said that these communities have, over a period of thirty years, had their Bali boundary fixed by Administrative Officers, and I am not convinced that there are any grounds — legal or equitable which would justify any readjustment of those boundaries. The Bafawchus and the Bametchoms and Bambutu and indeed the Bandes (Ngemba) plead insufficiency of land: "We are starving; we are suffering." I am not in a position to state whether that assertion is well founded or not. It was requested to visit portions of the land and I would have been willing to do so if the difficulty of obtaining transport had been less or if I had thought that a view of some of the areas alleged to be insufficient would have served any useful purpose. I did in fact get a general view of the area as the main road from Widikum-Bali-Bamenda passes through the land in dispute. A cursory view, however, would not put me in a position to give an opinion on the point. An opinion, to be of any value, could only be given after data and information had been obtained on such matters as the extent of the actual area occupied, the density of the population, the fertility of the soil, and whether the land available to these communities is being cultivated in the most husband-like manner. The point does not, in fact, arise at this Inquiry which is concerned with the rights of occupancy of the land in dispute. An alleged shortage of land by a Widikum community, if true, is not, in my opinion, a ground by itself for depriving the Bali people of their customary rights of occupancy or any rights of occupancy under the Land and Native Rights Ordinance.

I might point out that in the Bali clan area the population density is 107 persons per square mile whereas in Ngemba clan area which includes Bafawchu, Bametchom and Bambutu, the density is forty-two persons per square mile (see page 237 of Cameroons Report for 1950).

So far as the boundaries between the Balis and their Widikum neighbours outside the periphery are concerned, I submit for Your

Excellency's information a list of the Inquiries held and their dates:

Bambutu	Mr Hawkesworth (1921)
Bametchom	Dr Jeffreys (1942)
	Mr Brayne-Baker (1932)
Babad (Baba II)	Dr Jeffreys (1942)
Bafawchu	Mr Hawkesworth (1923)
	Mr J. S. Smith 1928)
	Mr Schofield (1938)
Pinyin	Mr J. S. Smith (1928)
Asong	Mr. J.S. Smith (1928)
Gujang (Moghamo)	M. J. S. Smith (1928)
Esum (Bamenjong)	M.L.Cantle1928)
Kai, Nya, Tunyang, Cobyang Meta	M. L. Cantle (1928)
Bande (Mankon)	Mr L. Cantle (1927)
	Mr Sharwood-Smith (1925)
	M. H. H. Marshall

I think it will be generally agreed that there must be some finality in the matter. It is essential that there shall be security of tenure; it is a condition precedent to orderly and progressive development. There can be no feeling of stability or security if boundaries are continually to be varied or sought to be varied. The complaints by the Widikum communities about these Inquiries are stereotyped; they allege that they were not present or were not given an opportunity of being heard or received no notice that an Inquiry was being held and that the findings were thus unfair and that Administrative Officers were prejudiced in favour of the Bali people. There is no substance in any of these complaints as is apparent when one refers to the appropriate files as I have done.

Further, it can be said, that, since the boundaries were fixed, there has been no trouble — except perhaps in the case of Bametchom — until just about the time when the present litigations were started when all the Widikum communities, realising, as the Bali spokesman had said, the value of unity, joined together to present a united front (see pages 66, 130). The Pinyins (South of

Plan) although not a nominal party to these actions are said to have made a monetary contribution. The Bali spokesman assured the Commission that the Pinyins and the Balis have no disputes at all. The Pinyins did not, in fact, take part in the recent disturbances. It is significant that the South-west Federation formed in 1949 just before the writs were issued includes the various Widikum communities, the Bali Native Authority being an enclave in their midst, the Balis remaining outside the Federation.

9. I wish to make some general observations. In my view, the Widikum communities both inside and outside the area bounded by the purple line, have been ill-advised, misguided and misled by unscrupulous agitators who have, for personal motives, persuaded the great majority of the simple Widikum people, by encouraging false hopes of re-acquiring all or a part of their land from the Balis, to contribute out of their slender means their small subscriptions of a shilling or two — I have seen the contributions book — towards the financing of litigation which, I am satisfied, is merely a speculative gamble and known to be such by those who have taken a principal part in instituting it. The Widikums have nothing to lose and everything to gain by instituting these proceedings. The Balis do not seek to upset the status quo or to extend their boundaries or encroach on Widikum land outside the purple line.

I regard it as essential that Your Excellency should inform the Widikum people that their claims to occupational rights over the area in dispute cannot be entertained as there are no grounds either legal or equitable or compassionate which justify any such rights being granted to them.

In my opinion, the acceptance by Government of the claims of the Widikum people either in whole or in part, will be regarded by them and others not only as an example of what may be gained by persistent petitioning and propaganda but also, to some extent, as a condonation of, if not a justification for, the recent disturbances which were created by the Widikum people. Other communities — neither Bali nor Widikum — are watching and waiting for the determination of the issues before this Inquiry in the expectation of a decision which will encourage them to commence similar actions against other defendants in the hope of ultimate benefit at the expense of their neighbours.

10. I have reached the following conclusions:

(1) That the Bali Nyonga people acquired by conquest the whole of the area verged purple about 1830 and have been in effective occupation of it since that date.

(2) That the Bali Nyongas have been, except for two claims by Mengen Mbos in 1921 and 1934, and some boundary adjustment, in unchallenged and undisturbed beneficial occupation of the said area for, at least, the last seventy-five years.

(3) That there are no grounds to support the allegations of the Widikum people that the boundaries between the Bali Nyongas and their Widikum neighbours round the periphery of the area verged purple were unfairly or improperly determined.

(4) That the Widikum peoples, resident and farming inside the said area, are not entitled to any rights of occupancy therein except those which the Fon of Bali permits them to enjoy, whether with or without payment of tribute or other conditions.

(5) That the Widikum communities outside the said area are not entitled to any rights of occupancy inside the said area and can only enjoy any such rights with the express permission of the Fon of Bali and subject to any conditions which he may think fit to impose.

(6) That there are no compassionate grounds — such as discriminatory treatment against, or unjust oppression of, Widikums by Bali Nyongas which, in justice, require that any Widikum people inside the area verged purple should have allotted to them inside the said area any special portion for their own exclusive beneficial enjoyment or which justify any readjustment of the Bali boundary verged purple.

11. I make the following recommendations:

(a) That the Widikum people who were the plaintiffs in those suits referred to in the terms of reference, shall be informed that their claims to a title, whether statutory or customary, to occupational rights in or over any portion of the area verged purple cannot be entertained. It will not be in my view, sufficient for Your Excellency merely to inform the Widikum communities as in (a) above. As security of tenure is indispensable to the future well-being, tranquillity and quiet, progressive development of the Bali people and with a view to the avoidance of continual friction with their Widikum neighbours in the years that lie ahead, it is essential that Your Excellency should make a formal positive declaration or acknowledgment to the effect that you deem it expedient that exclusive rights of occupancy over the land in dispute i.e. the area verged purple shall be vested in the Bali Nyonga people subject, at all times, to their native laws and customs and to the provisions of the Land and Native Rights Ordinance. I, therefore, recommend:

(b) That a declaration or acknowledgment to the above effect be made under section 4 of the Land and Native Rights Ordinance (Chapter 105). Subject to the opinion of your legal advisers, it seems to me that the sections 6, 7, 17, 20 of the Ordinance are not appropriate to the case of a native community and it is doubtful whether they were intended so to apply. (See Lord Lugard's "Dual Mandate" 1st Edition, page 292).

"Native" in section 2 means an individual and not a community. In practice Certificates of Occupancy are not granted even to individual native occupiers — a fortiori to native communities. It is quite inappropriate to refer to rent — whether by way of payment (section 7 Proviso) or exemption (section 20) — in such a case as the present occupation by the Bali Nyonga community of the area verged purple.

(c) That the boundaries demarcated by Administrative Officers either by consent or under the Inter-Tribal Boundaries Settlement Ordinance referred to in paragraph 8 shall not be disturbed on any ground which will appear to justify the criticism that they were illegally or unfairly or in any manner improperly determined.

(d) That if, at any future date, it becomes desirable, after full investigation, that there should be a boundary adjustment between the people of Bali and any of the Widikum communities now settled outside the area verged purple owing to the insufficiency of the land occupied by any such community, that there should be paid by Government to the Bali people compensation in respect of any portion of land inside the area verged purple of which the Bali people may in consequence be dispossessed.

12. This concludes my Report and Recommendation.

I have the honour to be,
Your Excellency's obedient Servant,

(Signed) A. G. B. MANSON, Commissioner

NOTE: *The Appendices and Plans mentioned in this Report have not been printed.*

Selected Bibliography

Official Publications

Croasdale, C.H., *Intelligence Report on the Bali*, 1932.

Ducan, N.C., *Report on the Bali Patrol*, Bamenda, 1920 Evans, G.V., *Annual Report for Bamenda Division*, 1923.

Hunt, W.E., *An Assessment Report on the Bali Clan in the Bamenda Division of Cameroons Province*, Bamenda, 1925.

Bamenda Divisional Reports, 1917 -1927.

Nigeria Gazette Extraordinary, n°45, vol. 39 and n°37 vol. 40 of 26 August 1952 and 8 August 1953 respectively.

Report on conditions in Bali Country, Bamenda, 2 February 1912.

Report of the Commission of Inquiry under the Inter-tribal Boundaries Settlement Ordinance, Bamenda, March 1949.

Books

Abubakar, Sa'ad. *The Lamibe of Fombina: A Political history of the Adamawa 1809-1901*, (London: OUP, 1977).

Anene, J. C., *The International Boundaries of Nigeria*, (London: Longman, 1970).

Chilver, Elizabeth M., *Zintgraff's Explorations in Bamenda*, (Buea: Government Printer, 1966).

Frobenius, Leo, *Und Afrika Sprach*, (Berlin: Vita Deutsches Verlaghaus, 1913)

Garbosa, Bitemya Sambo, *Labarum Chambawa da A l'Amuransa*, (Historical Society of Nigeria, 1960).

Hutter, Franz, *Wanderungen and Forschungen in Nord-Hinterland von Kamerun*, (Braunschweig: 1902).

Kaberry and Chilver, *Traditional Bamenda* (Buea: Government Printer, 1967).

Meek, C.K. *Tribal Studies in Northern Nigeria*, (London: Kegan Paul, Trench and Trubner, 1931).

Mohammadou, Eldridge, *Les Royaumes Foulbe du Plateau de l'Adamaoua au*

XIXe siècle (Tokyo: Institute for the Study of Languages and Cultures of Africa and Asia, 1978).

Ritzenthaler, Pat, *The Fon of Bafut*, (London: Cassel, 1966).

Rudin, Harry, *Germans in the Cameroons, 1884-1914*, (London: Jonathan Cape, 1983).

Tardits, Claude, *Le Royaume Bamoun*, (Paris: Armand Colin, 1980).

Zintgraff, Eugen, *Nord Kamerun* (Berlin, 1895).

Articles

Chilver, Elizabeth M., "A Bamileke Community in Bali Nyonga: A note on the Bawok", *African Studies*, 23, n°3-4, 1964.

Fardon, Richard, "A chronology of Pre-Colonial Chamba History", *Paideuma*, 29, 1983.

Jeffreys, M.D.W, "Traditional Sources prior to 1890 for the Grassfields Bali of Northwestern Cameroons", *Africa und Ubersee*, Band XLVI/4 1963.

Kaberry and Chilver, "An Outline of the traditional political system of Bali Nyonga."

Moisel, Max, "Ein Expedition in die Grashochlander Mittel-Kamerun", *Deutsche Kolonialzeitung*, n°15, 11 April 1908.

Moisel, Max, "Zur Geschichte von Bali und Barnum': *Globus*, vol. 93.

Unpublished works

Chilver, Elizabeth M., *Diary on Bali Nyonga*, Ms, 1960.

Chilver, Elizabeth M., *The Bali Chamba of West Cameroon, Report to the Bali History Committee*, Ms, 1960.

Fardon, Richard, *The Chamba: A Comparative History of Tribal Politics*, Ph.D. Thesis, University of London, 1980.

Jeffreys, M.D.W, *Tribal notes on the Bamenda Grassfields*, Ms, 1951.

Kaberry, P.M. *Fieldnotes on Bali Nyonga*, Ms, 1960.

Njoya, Sultan, *Histoire et coutume Bamoun*, Memoire de l'IFAN, Yaounde, 1972.

Warnier, J.P., *Sociologie du Bamenda Pre-Colonial*, These de Doctorat, Universite de Paris X, 1983.

Index

Abakpa 129, 130, 133
Abramowski 89
Abumbi I 66, 68
Adama, Modibo 4
Adamawa 4, 155
Adametz 74, 88
Ahidjo, President 114, 115
Alantika mountains 1, 2
alliances 7, 48, 50, 104
Anglo-French Commission 55
Armstrong, Captain 94
Ayissi Mvodo, Victor 115

Baaku 53
Babadju 13, 71, 82, 85
Babessong 50
Babungo 50, 77
Baforchu 32, 42, 43, 49, 50, 68, 71,
    85, 89, 102, 104
Bafou-Fondong 16, 17, 19, 24, 30,
    40, 41
Bafreng 13, 31, 32, 33, 40, 50, 51,
    52, 53, 113
Bafut 13, 31, 32, 38, 50, 65, 66, 67,
    68, 69, 70, 77, 79, 140, 144,
    156
Bagam 19, 21, 31, 47, 77
Bali-Bamun War v, 26
Bali chiefdoms
    Bali Gangsin 6, 21, 112
    Bali Gasho 6, 17, 20, 21, 112

Bali Gham 6, 19, 20, 21, 96, 112
Bali Konntan 21, 30, 32, 33, 34,
    43
Bali Kumbat 6, 20, 21, 27, 31, 32,
    35, 38, 51, 52, 53, 54, 112,
    138, 139, 144
Bali Muti 21, 25, 112
Bali Nyonga ii, iii, iv, v, vi, vii, 6,
    7, 19, 21, 23, 24, 25, 26, 27,
    28, 30, 31, 32, 33, 34, 35, 36,
    37, 38, 39, 40, 41, 42, 43, 44,
    45, 46, 47, 48, 49, 50, 51, 52,
    53, 54, 56, 58, 59, 60, 63, 65,
    70, 72, 73, 74, 75, 77, 78, 80,
    82, 84, 85, 86, 87, 88, 89, 91,
    92, 96, 97, 98, 100, 103, 109,
    110, 111, 112, 113, 114, 115,
    116, 117, 118, 119, 135, 138,
    139, 144, 145, 146, 147, 148,
    152, 153, 156, 163
Bali Kumbat-Bali Nyonga War 52,
    53
Bali Native Authority 123, 131,
    134, 151
Bali Nyonga in German Policy vi,
    63
Bali-Widikum rapprochement 109,
    110
Bambalang 50
Bambili 31
Bambui 13, 31, 51
Bambuliwe 52
Bambunji 49, 71, 72, 92

Bambutu 51, 140, 144, 149, 150
Bamelike 43
Bamenda v, 1, 5, 6, 8, 9, 11, 12, 24,
  25, 31, 32, 35, 36, 42, 43, 44,
  47, 51, 52, 53, 55, 56, 58, 59,
  60, 62, 63, 65, 66, 69, 70, 72,
  74, 77, 79, 81, 82, 83, 84, 86,
  88, 89, 91, 92, 93, 94, 95, 96,
  97, 101, 102, 103, 104, 106,
  110, 111, 113, 116, 118, 121,
  122, 123, 124, 125, 126, 128,
  129, 130, 131, 132, 133, 134,
  135, 139, 145, 148, 149, 155,
  156
Bamenda Declaration of 1912 84
Bamenjong 49, 50, 71, 72, 92, 140,
  150
Bamessing 50
Bamessinge 49, 50, 71, 82, 85
Bamessong 49, 56, 71, 85
Bamileke 9, 17, 26, 28, 43, 44, 91,
  117, 156
Bamumbu 82, 84
Bamun v, 9, 10, 11, 12, 24, 25, 26,
  27, 28, 31, 35, 39, 43, 80, 91,
  99, 101
Bamungen 43, 104, 105
Bamunyi 13, 15, 49, 71, 85
Bandem 27
Bangang 71, 82
Bangante 25, 26, 44, 117
Banggola 31
Bangu 28, 29
Banja 71, 72, 94
Bansoa 25, 26, 43, 50
Bănten 12, 21, 27, 29, 35, 38
Banyang 74
Banyo 6, 8, 9, 35, 71, 82
Bari 8
Basel Mission College 97, 99, 119
Basler Mission 75, 77
Basler missionaries 60, 75

Bata 3, 4, 5
BaTi v, 11, 12, 24, 25, 27, 28, 43
Batibo 49, 71, 84, 121, 122, 127
Bawock 117, 118. *See also* Bawok
Bawok 44, 47, 156
Benue plains 5
Benue River 37
Berlin Conference 55
bĕdmfòn 30, 38, 39
Bikom 13, 31, 32
blacksmiths 2, 32
blood brotherhood 60
Bossa 43, 71, 72, 95, 106
boundaries 55, 84, 101, 114, 115,
  123, 140, 143, 149, 150, 151,
  152, 153
Britain 87, 88, 94
British Administration 145
British Cameroons 91, 100, 112,
  163
British soldiers 89, 94
Buea 8, 56, 63, 84, 113, 125, 155
burial 41, 97
Buti 6, 8, 9, 12, 29

Cameroon ii, 1, 7, 52, 74, 84, 113,
  114, 116, 119, 135, 156, 163
Catechist Training Centre 77
Chamba v, 1, 2, 3, 4, 5, 6, 7, 8, 9,
  10, 11, 12, 13, 15, 16, 17, 18,
  19, 20, 21, 23, 24, 25, 30, 34,
  35, 36, 40, 41, 42, 43, 50, 51,
  52, 110, 112, 156, 163
Chamba Daka 1, 2
Chamba Leko 1, 2, 3, 5, 6, 7, 9
Chang Division 84
Chang plateau 16
Chief of Nkwen
  Azefor II 54
Chilver, E.M. 7, 8, 9, 11, 13, 19, 25,

27, 32, 35, 38, 44, 52, 53, 56, 71, 74, 81, 85, 116, 155, 156
chĭntèd 28, 46, 56
Chomba 51, 117
  Bamechom (also known as) 49, 51, 85
Christianity 75, 76
Christmas 66
colonial administration 70, 81, 86, 98
colonial policy 69, 85
condominium 90
conspiracy 66, 80
Crookenden, Major 88, 93
customs 109, 146, 148, 153

dane guns 37, 38, 41, 57, 106
Demsa 3
Diddo 3, 4
diet 15
Dingbula 47
Dip 29
diplomacy 7, 84
Dobell, Major General 88, 89, 90
Doh Gashu II 20
Douala 58, 69, 71, 88, 89
drought 5
Duncan, N.C. 92, 94

Ebermaier, Governor 83, 84, 85, 86, 87, 89
Endeley, Dr. E.M.L. 113
Ernst, Ferdinand 65, 75, 76, 80, 82
Esser, Max 73, 75
Evans, G.V. 97, 102, 155

famine 5

farming 26, 103, 143, 145, 148, 152
Faro-Deo 1, 5, 7, 14, 21
Fatfat 53
flag 4, 33, 34, 67
Fofuleng 29
Fogako 34
Fokunyang 34
Fomenjeng, subchief 29
Fomukong, Chief 52, 67
Fomunyam 29
Foncha, J.N. 113
Fongwe 27, 72
Fontem 16
fòntə' 28, 29, 30, 34, 38, 46
Fonyonga I 10, 23, 24, 31, 37, 38, 40, 43, 52
Fonyonga II 40, 41, 42, 43, 46, 47, 50, 68, 70, 71, 74, 79, 82, 84, 88, 94, 96, 97, 98, 99, 117
Fonyonga's Reforms v, 28
forced labour 80, 83, 86
Fortingo, Robert 113
Fosang 29
Fosangam 29
Fowon 29
France 87, 90, 91
Franco-British condominium 90
Franco-British Declaration on the Cameroons 91
French Equatorial Africa 87
friendship 42, 47, 50, 54, 57, 58, 59, 62, 65, 68, 70, 78, 79, 80, 92, 99, 141
Fulani 3, 4, 5, 8
Fuleng 11, 27
Fumban 6, 10, 11, 12, 24, 26, 27, 77, 82

Gabana 15, 16
Gabanjang 7

Gagwanyin 52, 53, 54
GaKonntan 21
Galabe II 20
Galanga 19, 20, 21
Galega I 35, 37, 38, 40, 42, 43, 46,
    47, 48, 50, 57, 59, 62, 64, 68,
    75, 76, 78
Galega II vi, 54, 98, 99, 100, 111,
    113, 116, 117, 119
Galim mountains 8
Gangsin 6, 7, 21, 112
Ganyam 7, 21
Ganyonga III 113, 117, 119
Gashaka 10
Gatkuna 2
Gavabe 20, 21
Gawolbe v, vii, 1, 6, 7, 8, 9, 10, 11,
    12, 13, 14, 15, 16, 17, 18, 19,
    20, 21, 23, 24, 27, 30, 36, 40,
    41, 42, 43
George V, King 89
German administration 72, 85, 104
German Colonial Office 58, 84
Germany
    German resistance 88, 89
gilìgwa 41
Glauning, Captain Hans 71, 81, 82
Goksela 19, 35
Goodliffe, F.A. 104, 105, 106, 107,
    122, 135, 136, 138, 140, 141,
    143, 145
Guzang 49, 71, 85, 93, 117
Gwaabe 29
Gwananji 29
Gwanchelleng 29
Gwandi 29
Gwayebit 29
gwè 39
Gyando 9, 13

Hawkesworth, Mr. 102, 150
House of Chiefs 100, 113
human resources 58
Hummel, Ms 77
Hunt, W.E. 25, 42, 72, 88, 89, 92,
    93, 94, 96, 102, 122, 140,
    141, 142, 145, 147, 155
Hutter, Lieutenant Franz 64, 155

Inter-Bali Rivalries v, 51
Inter-Tribal Boundaries Settlement
    Ordinance 123, 135, 154
ivory 50, 58, 66, 69, 78, 81

Jantzen and Thormahlen 60, 66
Jeffreys, M.D.W. 19, 25, 31, 52, 150,
    156
jihad 4, 5

Kaberry, P.M. 7, 8, 13, 21, 34, 38,
    52, 85, 155, 156
Kamerun 55, 57, 58, 59, 61, 62, 64,
    69, 70, 72, 73, 87, 88, 89, 90,
    91, 112, 113, 155, 156
Kamerun National Democratic
    Party 113
Keller 75
Keninga Tashim 49
king-makers 20
kola nuts 12, 50
Kolm v, 16, 17, 19, 21, 22, 25
Kolongti, Lake 7
Koncha 3, 5, 7, 8, 9
Konntan 21, 30, 32, 33, 34, 35, 43
Kovifem 9
kɔm 46
kɔmmfòn 28, 29, 30
Kufad 6, 8, 9, 12, 29

Kufom 34, 35, 38, 40, 42, 52
Kumchu 44
Kumpi 27
Kundem 11, 27
Kungwe 49
Kunyang 32, 42, 145
Kuti 11, 12, 24, 25, 26, 27, 35, 43
Kwen 27, 29
Kwifon 43, 50

Lamurde Jungum 1, 4, 5
Lancaster House Conference 112
Land and Native Rights Ordinance
    137, 149, 153
land disputes 81, 114, 135
languages 1, 25
    Daka 1, 2
    Leko 1, 2, 3, 5, 6, 7, 9
    Mungaka 25, 77, 78, 80
Lap 11, 27, 29
leadership 10, 11, 14, 17, 20, 30, 38,
    46, 47, 98, 108, 110, 114
Lebaga, W.P. 113
Leimbacher 75
Lela 31, 33, 117
LoLo 12

Mambila 10
Màmfòn 24
manded 38
Manjɔŋ 30
Manjɔŋs 38, 67
Mankon 43, 50, 51, 52, 54, 65, 66,
    67, 68, 69, 70, 79, 143, 150
Mankon War, The 65
Manson, Justice A.G.B. vi, 107,
    108, 109, 114
martyrdom 69
Mbatu 51, 68, 71, 85

Mbelu 43
Mbengwi 77, 122, 127, 128
Mbufung 43, 143, 145, 147
Mbum people 8
Mbuombuo, King 10, 11, 26, 27, 31
Meek, C.K. 1, 155
Menchum Falls 69
Menemo 36, 95, 122, 123, 124, 126,
    127, 128, 129, 130, 133, 134,
    144
Menemo Intelligence Report 122
Mengen Mbo 126, 127, 128, 129,
    135, 136, 137, 141, 144, 146,
    148
Mengen Muwa 126, 127, 128, 129,
    145, 146, 147, 148
Menzel, Captain 81, 82
Meta 13, 32, 33, 34, 36, 42, 43, 49,
    50, 72, 73, 85, 93, 94, 96,
    100, 101, 102, 103, 104, 105,
    106, 107, 108, 109, 115, 116,
    117, 150
mfòntə' 28, 29, 34
migration 2, 3, 5, 6, 7, 12, 13, 14,
    21
military lodges 30
military tactics 30
mock fighting 31
Modi 21
Moghamo 35, 109, 121, 122, 123,
    124, 125, 126, 127, 128, 129,
    130, 133, 134, 140, 144, 150
Moghamo Intelligence Report 122
Moghamo Native Court 121
Mohammadou, Eldridge 1, 3, 7, 8,
    9, 10, 155
Moisel, Max 64, 65, 72, 76, 156
Mount Djoumbal 9
mounted raiders 6
Mubako 25, 40, 54, 117
Muna, Solomon Tandeng 116, 141,
    146, 147

Mundame-Bali route 58
Mundi, Regina 113
Mungen Mbu 49, 104, 106, 117
Munyam 11, 27

Nahnyonga 21, 23, 24
Nana, Chief 44, 47
Native Authorities 96
  Native Authority school 96
Native Authority 96, 113, 122, 123,
  131, 134, 151
native laws 153
Nchamukong, J.T. 113
Ndagambila 6, 7, 12, 21, 28, 30
ndâle 38
ndanjem 38
Ndâŋgɔ' 38
Ndifon Gwansalla, Reverend Elisa
  78
Ndiyang 11, 27, 29
Ndop 31, 50
Ndudina, Doh 56
Ngaoundere 8
Ngemba 35, 109, 121, 122, 123,
  124, 125, 126, 127, 128, 129,
  130, 133, 134, 139, 140, 144,
  149
Ngemba Native Court 121, 127,
  128
Nggod 27
Nggonlan 31
Ngiam 35, 42
Ngie 13
Ngod 11
Ngufor I 13
Ngu Moonzi, Chief 10, 11
Ngwa'ndikang 52
Nigeria vi, 1, 21, 55, 87, 90, 91,
  105, 107, 109, 110, 112, 113,
  114, 121, 125, 129, 133, 135,

  155
Calabar 50, 58, 105
Njimonikam 47
Njoya, Sultan 99
Nkoumelap 25
Northern Cameroons 112
Noun, River 12, 24, 25, 27, 31
Nsa'ra 10
Nso 9
Nsongwa 51, 67
Ntânbèd 39, 67
Nyasoso 77
Nyongpasi 21, 23. See also Fon-
  yonga I
Nzi Mayup 11

oral traditions 6, 19

Palace retainers 28
Palmer Judgement 106
Palmer, Justice 105, 106
palm wine 26, 60
patronage 28, 76
Pavel 69
Pefok, I.F. 7, 15, 113
Peli 8, 20, 21, 29, 30
Picot, Georges 90
Pinyin 34, 35, 37, 49, 50, 71, 85,
  140, 150
plebiscite 112, 113
Podevin 91, 92, 94, 139
Puttkamer, Governor 70

queen mother 24

regnal name 21, 23, 117

Rifum 10
royal authority 41
royal medicines 28
Russia 87

Sabum, Michael 113
Salisbury, Lord 55
Samsu 19, 20, 21
Sang 11
Sangaam 11, 27
Santa 19, 129, 130, 133, 134
Schuler 75
Seitz, Governor 82
Set 11, 27
slaves 50
Sokoto 4
Southern Cameroons 112, 113,
    114. See also British Cam-
    eroons
Spellenberg 75
Sprangenberg, Lt. von 68
sub-chiefs 30, 47, 95
suzerainty 40, 42, 79, 80, 81, 85, 92,
    94, 95, 98, 101, 138, 142

Tadkon 105, 110
tădmànjì vii, 40, 48, 49, 50, 62, 71,
    79, 83
Takum 13
Tali 15
tax 61, 70, 71, 72, 73, 78, 80, 81, 83,
    84, 85, 94, 95, 131
Tchu'ako 32, 33, 34
Tibati 6, 8, 12
Tikali 6, 9, 12, 29
Tikar 9, 10
Ti-Mbundam 43, 44, 47
Tita Fofam 49, 50
Tita Fokum 49, 50

Tita Fongwa 53
Tita Fonja 38
Tita Gwandiku 29
Tita Gwenjang 38, 40, 49, 67, 68,
    99
Tita Kuna 29, 30
Tita Ladinga 38, 49
Tita Lavod 38, 40, 49
Tita Mbo 40
Tita Mongu 38
Tita Mufut 49
Tita Nji 7, 38, 40, 49, 67
Tita Nyambi 99
Tita Sikod Foncham 49
Trans-African Highway 119
tributary villages 49, 50
tribute 4, 35, 40, 42, 48, 50, 80, 116,
    139, 152
tutuwàn 33, 34, 67

United Kingdom 90, 135, 141
United Nations 141, 142

Vai boys 66
Vanigansen, Mochiggle 113
vassal villages 44, 73, 79, 82, 93
Vertue, Captain 94
Vielhauer, Reverend Adolf 77, 78
Vincent Samdala, Prince 98
Vòma 46, 118
Von Sommerfeld 88

War Council 30, 34, 38, 39, 46, 67
Warnier, J.P. 9, 13, 54, 156
Weber, Miss Lina 77
Widikum 35, 36, 39, 42, 43, 67, 68,
    72, 80, 101, 104, 105, 106,
    107, 108, 109, 110, 111, 114,

117, 130, 133, 135, 136, 137,
138, 139, 140, 141, 142, 143,
144, 145, 146, 147, 148, 149,
150, 151, 152, 153, 154
Women Teachers Training Centre
77. *See also* Weber, Lina
Wum 13

Zintgraff, Eugen vi, 47, 56, 57, 58,
59, 60, 61, 62, 64, 65, 66, 67,
68, 70, 73, 74, 76, 85, 140,
141, 142, 155, 156
Zintgraff - Galega Treaty 61

By the same Author

The Bali Chamba of Cameroon
The Making of a Fondom
To Seek a Better Life
The Politics of the British Cameroons Plebiscites
Points of Light in Bali Nyonga History